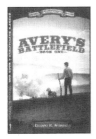 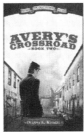 

Don't miss any of Deanna K. Klingel's

amazing novels.

All her novels are available on

Amazon.com and Kindle ebooks.

Personal Facebook page is Deanna K. Klingel

Facebook for books: Books by Deanna

Webpage: www.booksbydeanna.com

Email: deannaklingel@yahoo.com

1

Rock and a Hard Place

To Mary Ann

ROCK AND A HARD PLACE

A Lithuanian Love Story

Su Dievu

Deanna K. Klingel

Deanna K. Klingel

This is a creative work by Deanna K. Klingel. The family is real. So is the story.

Shari Parker Publishing and Printing
2785 CR 3103
New Boston, Texas 75570
903-933-6273
sharipar@yahoo.com
www.shariparkerpublishingandprinting.com

Printed in the United States of America

Deanna K. Klingel

Table of Contents

Rock and a Hard Place

Deanna K. Klingel

Acknowledgements

Thank you to Donna and Vytas for sharing their love stories. It required an intimate trust that I appreciate. I've tried to tell their stories without invading their privacy unnecessarily. Some of the stories they've not told before, or even shared with each other. The process of dredging up the past, recreated nightmares and unpleasant memories for them, as well as rediscovering joys of their childhood. They both have amazing memories embroidered with the smallest and sweetest details. I'm grateful to Donna and Vytas for sharing their wonderful memories and histories, both pleasant and unpleasant.

The stories of our histories, our own biographies, must be told to new generations. We all learn from our past. Edmund Burke said, "Those who do not know history are destined to repeat it." Young people need to know these things happened, how, and why. Our future depends on it. Our youngsters must learn to speak out against injustices or they will live in tyranny; it's the lesson of history.

Keeping journals and diaries of your lives now can be shared with your own descendants who will thank you for that. I encourage you readers to be the writers of your own stories. Thanks to the thousands of immigrants who brought to our shores the work ethic of their homelands and their era. It was you who made America great. It was you who made America's work force the best in the world. It is for you that the Statue of Liberty stands so tall and proud.

Thanks to Charlene Homolka for the first read, and to the rest of my Cashiers Writing Group for their patience and insight.

Thank you, Dave, my constant encouragement and influencer, for support of all my work.

To Shari Parker, editor and her team at Shari Parker Publishing my gratitude for publishing the story of Donna and Vytas.

Deanna K. Klingel

Dedicated to the memory of the men and women who suffered and lost so much during the long struggle for freedom and autonomy in the Baltic nations, and to the next generation of Americans who must learn from those who were there.

Rock and a Hard Place

Lithuania's Children

To understand Vytas' and Danute's story, we must understand their time and place. For centuries the small Baltic country of Lithuania has been in the middle of various power plays; between a rock and a hard place, as the saying goes.

Lithuania is a coastal country with a seaport viable year round. This is of great value to countries that are landlocked or frozen for long winters. Take a look at a map or globe and you'll see why this small country was, and is, important to larger, more powerful countries.

From 1795, until the Bolshevik Revolution in 1918, Lithuania wasn't a country but a governate of Czarist Russia. When the Russian Czar outlawed the Lithuanian language and burned all the books written in Lithuanian, the Lithuanians began uprising. How would you feel if strangers took over your house, made your language illegal? You could go to jail, or be shot for using your native language. Can you even imagine such a thing?

Lithuania declared her independence from Russia in 1918, and battled to secure it in 1920. Between 1920 and 1940, between the two world wars, Lithuania was a free, independent, and prosperous country.

In 1930, on a large and comfortable farm in the small rural bergen of Vepriai, Vytautas, called Vytas, was born to Jonas the Bergenmeister and his wife, Sofia. The Bergenmeister is the equivalent of a mayor in America. Forty miles away, in Lithuania's second largest city of Kaunas, Danute was born into a pharmacist-army officer's family, the daughter of Petras and Anele.

Both children grew up traditionally, one in the city, one on a farm. Danute and Vytas were typical of the young people growing up in that time, in that place. This is their story, which is also Lithuania's story. They were all caught between a rock and a hard place.

Vytas 1930s

Chapter 1

Homeland

"1930, our lucky year." Jonas smiled at his wife Sofia, who beamed a tired but happy smile at her husband.

"Yes, so lucky, and so blessed. We have so much to be thankful for, dear Jonas." She laid her head back on her damp, rumpled pillow.

"This is the 500-year anniversary of the Grand Duke of Lithuania. We should name our new son after him, what do you say to that?" Jonas asked.

"I say Vytautas is a good name for the Bergenmeister's son. So he shall be baptized Vytautas then. We shall tell the priest." She smiled at her children gathered around her bedside watching the new baby suckle.

"Probably he will guess already. Lots of boys born in 1930 will have the name Vytautas, I imagine," Jonas said.

"Probably true, but it's still a good name," she replied. The children nodded in agreement.

Vincas, ten years old, stood close. Still dressed in his school clothes, short pants, suspenders, white shirt, bow tie, felted jacket, he contemplated his position in the family as Baby Vytas's big brother. He nervously fingered his cap in his hands and moved even closer to the bed for a better look at the newest family member.

Eight year-old Jane studied the tiny red baby. The family lived in a sprawling house with large rooms all on one floor. She looked around her.

"I guess there will be room for our little brother," she decided.

Two year-old Jonas, Jr., called Jon, sucked his thumb. He wasn't sure about any of this. He studied the dresser drawer lined with flannel for the baby's bed. He wanted to lie beside his mother, where the baby now slumbered. Grandfather sucked on his favorite pipe and patted Jon's small shoulders reassuringly.

"What do you think, little Jon?" he asked. Jon stared wide-eyed at his grandfather.

"We can always use another boy on the farm," his big brother Vincas encouraged him.

"Ja," said his father, nodding. "Always room for another."

The house had been built in the previous year of logs covered in wood plank on the outside. The rooms were so large, the ceiling so high, it was impossible to keep the house warm in the winter. The attached barn for the animals helped to heat the house. In summer the pleasant breezes cooled the large, open rooms. The boys grew up together on the large cattle and grain farm.

Vytas grew strong and tall quickly. He slept with his brothers under the galvanized sheet metal roof, and walked three and a half miles to school with them as soon as he turned six years old. They attended public school, but since all the students were Catholic, the Catechism was as much a part of the school curriculum as math and composition. He worked alongside his brothers, farmers, and hired hands on the farm, never venturing too far away. As the farmers' seasons came and went, Vytas grew and learned.

"You boys carry this pipe to the fireplace. It will connect the wooden tub I made to the fireplace. The water in the tub will be hot from the fire and the air will be steamy when we throw dippers of water against the hot stones."

The boys listened to their father's instructions. They hefted the pipe, and hauled it into the huge out building that was heated by a large stone fireplace. Their father had crafted the 4' X 4' wooden tub near the fireplace. The boys struggled through the door, and dropped their load near the tub before heading back to the stone pile.

"You're getting strong, boys," their father complimented them.

Dropping an armload of stone, and wiping the sweat from his face, Vytas asked, "Why does it have to be so big, Dad?"

"Not too many people have a sauna. It's a special thing we will have when we are finished. I want it to be big enough so we can share our sauna with guests. We must always share our good fortune, ja?"

The family all worked together shaping the cement tiles to cover the roof of their sauna. "This is another good skill for you boys to learn, eh? Making fine roof tiles can be a good living someday." The boys looked at each other, rolled their eyes and smiled.

"Ja, Dad; another good skill."

"The more skills you learn, the more jobs you can have when you are men. When you can work, you'll not go hungry. I want you always to be able to care for yourselves and your families. It means you have pride, and your work is pleasing to God."

When the sauna was finished, Jonas launched the family into another project.

"We will disassemble the neighbor's grain storage barn and move it to our farm," he explained.

"Why are we doing this? We already have a big grain storage barn," questioned Vytas.

"Ja, we do. We can use another. And our neighbors need money more than grain storage right now."

"Oh. I see." Vytas was nodding his head, slowly getting the gist of what his father was doing. The owners of the grain storage barn had disappeared one night. Some of their relatives had come to care for the animals and to try to get the family's affairs taken care of. They were selling the stock and furnishings. Perhaps they could use the money to help their relatives, or buy food for them. His father was helping. The Russians now held that farm.

"Do you think the neighbors will ever come back, Vincus?" Vytas asked his brother.

"Only God knows, I think."

Vytas loved their farm: the frosted breath of the cattle in the winter, the companionable dogs, the smell of hay, the ripened grain shimmering under the summer sun, the wagons, the pulling-team of six, the sound of the rain on the metal roof; the smell of his mother's cooking, the laughter of his brothers and Jane and the cry of their newest baby sister. It was all a happy home for Vytas.

In his daily prayers he thanked God that he'd been born on the farm and not in the city. He didn't mind walking to his country school. He found and identified the native plants along the way. He picked up interesting sticks and twigs to craft into intricate shapes that decorated the barns and walls with interesting designs. He crafted gifts from wood and nature for his family, friends, and neighbors. He made decorations for his mother's gardens out of things he collected in the woods and in the fields.

He didn't worry that when he went to high school he'd be ten miles from home, riding a narrow gauge train every day. He'd face that when it happened. For now he enjoyed his farm life. But he wondered about the missing neighbors.

"No one will take our farm away from us, will they, Dad? The Russians won't bother us, will they?"

No one answered him, so he took that as an affirmation and breathed a sigh of relief.

Chapter 2

Barn Diving

"That's it then. That's the last of the feed stores to be stacked. Let's go celebrate!" Vincus called. The tired boys wiped the sweat off their faces with their kerchiefs. Vincus put away the tools.

"I'm already too tired," complained Jon.

"Come on, Jon, it's time for some fun. Meet us in the barn, Vincus," Vytas called.

The boys ran into the huge granary and scampered up the girders as athletic and lithe as barn cats.

"Come along, Jon, you're poky. Come practice your dives," teased Vytas. The boys crawled out onto the rafters looking down on a sea of barley bundles.

"I've already practiced. I can do two somersaults in the air now," Jon replied.

"Two? Really? Show us, master diver."

Jon walked out on the rafter, arms out to his side, one foot in front of the other like a tight rope performer in the circus. Out on the center of the beam he turned frontward, pointed his arms above him and leapt out, tucking his legs into a tight ball, somersaulting twice before landing with a deadly thump. Jon hung over a lower beam that had been hidden just under the bales.

"Jon!" Vytas and Vincas screamed and clamored down the girders. They crawled across the heap of barley bales where their brother dangled silently with his arms and legs sprawled across the bales of grain.

The boys stared at their motionless brother. Vytas's heart hammered, but he couldn't utter a word.

"God, he's dead," breathed Vincas. "No, oh God, no."

"Jon, Jonas...wake up. Don't die, Jon, you can't die. Wake up Jonas!" stammered Vytas.

"Why can't I die? Just because you said so?" Jon coughed and rubbed his sore ribs. "You aren't in charge of everything, Vytas." He groaned and sat up.

"You're alive?" Vincas breathed a huge sigh and collapsed onto the barley bales. "Thank God, you are alive."

"Of course I'm alive," he coughed.

Jon struggled to sit up. Vytas offered a hand and helped him stand. In the waning afternoon light, the three brothers stood in awkward silence.

"I'm glad you're alive, Jonas," said Vincas solemnly.

"And I," added Vytas.

"Ja. Me too. Next time, I will check the depth of the beam before I do *three* somersaults," Jon laughed.

"Ja. Next time we'll all do that," agreed Vytas. The boys wrapped their arms around their brother's shoulders and walked unsteadily back to the house. Jon gently massaged his sore ribs.

"Are you going to tell Mother?" Jon whispered.

"Tell her what?" shrugged Vincus.

Autumn moved quickly into winter in Lithuania. Winter came hard and brutally cold.

Chapter 3

Gravel Pit Skiing

The wind howled. The boys lowered their heads and bent into the gusts.

"There are places in Spain, I hear, where the summer never ends," called Jon over his shoulder. "Not like our cruel Lithuanian winters with temperatures dropping to 40 degrees below zero. Probably in Spain they don't wear all these clothes. Maybe they are barefooted even in the winter. I'm going to go there someday."

"Where'd you hear all that?" Vytas's voice was muffled behind his scarf.

Bundled in sheepskin coats over the top of their heavily layered clothing, they walked as fast as possible through the snow with their felt boots rubbing against their knees, the rubber soles cutting through the snow. The friction of the woolen socks their mother knitted rubbed blisters on their heels. Vytas and his brothers walked three and a half miles to school and three and a half miles back while darkness descended at four in the afternoon.

Gathered around the table for supper, the red-cheeked farm boys talked amiably with their parents.

"I hear our two big rooms at the school are too full for us now," said Vytas.

"It's good of the town people to offer their unused buildings for extra school rooms," said his mother.

"But, it looks like school will be held in three different places. Now there will be five men to teach us," added Jon. Their conversation was interrupted by passing food dishes, and compliments to the cook.

"So, Vytas, I see your school group has been moved. Now you'll have an extra mile to walk. You'll need to leave earlier than the rest of us and walk alone," said Vincas.

Vytas moaned. "Ja, that's so. I'll be getting up earlier, and the walk will be lonely."

"I have a better idea," said their father. "You can all leave a bit earlier, and Vytas can take the last mile faster. You'll split the difference, and Vytas doesn't have to go it alone."

"That's a good idea," agreed Vincus. "I vote for that plan."

"A good brother." Their father raised his water glass in salute to his sons.

"What is the temperature gauge on the barn reading?" The boys asked the question anxiously every morning, hoping to hear "fourteen below."

"Is it minus fourteen degrees yet?"

"Please be cold today," they wished loudly.

"As soon as that old mercury dips to fourteen degrees below zero, out will come the sleds and my new skiis!" Vytas pressed his face against the frosty window and peered out at the thermometer on the barn.

"Yeah, no school. Please, please be fourteen below today!"

Vytas' skis were both cross country and downhill skis, since the boys really didn't know the difference. They'd never seen "real" skiers. Vytas's skis had been crafted by a man in town who knew how to make skis. Vytas tried once to ski cross-country to school but it took him so long he was tardy for class.

"That was my first and last time to try that," he apologized to his teacher, who laughed and understood.

Vytas, his brothers, their cousin Robert, and friends gathered at the gravel pit to try out Vytas' new skis when the first snow covered the ground, and the temperature plummeted to that magical fourteen degree below, locking the school door.

"You go first, Vytas, and show us how to do this."

"Ja, sure. It's my first time down this hill, too," he reminded them. "But, I think I have a good idea."

Deanna K. Klingel

He buckled the straps over the skis and over his boots. The boys pulled him to the edge of the precipice which was covered in a thin layer of snow. The skis scraped on the gravel as he pushed them along on his feet. He fearlessly looked over the edge at the steep incline and the sudden upturn at the bottom. The hill was a giant letter U.

"This is good," Jon said. "When you get to the bottom you'll go right back up. It's a good way to get back up to the top and stop, don't you think?"

"Ja, I think so, too." Everyone agreed that was the most sensible way to get back up the hill.

"We'll count to three and give you a push," their cousin said.

"One-two-three—ugh" they gave him a shove down the hill. The gravel under the thin snow scraped and screeched while the boys cheered. Vytas was at the bottom in a second, still standing. The hill leveled out. The gravel wall reared up in front of him. Vytas gasped. The skis stabbed into the gravel wall. Vytas yelled and thrust his hands out in front of him. The skis made a loud crack and his feet shot out of the skis. Vytas smashed into the wall.

The boys charged to the bottom of the hill.

"Well, looks like that didn't work so well," sighed Jon, holding the broken pieces of skis.

"You okay?" asked Robert.

"Ja. I'm fine," Vytas answered with disgust. He didn't like looking foolish.

"You don't look too fine," said Jon. The boys stared as the blood dripped from Vytas' red nose. The imprint of the gravel left a track mark across his face.

"I think you might have a shiner coming on," warned Vincas.

"Worse. My skis are broken."

Chapter 4

Machination of the Devil

In the long winter evenings when darkness began in the afternoon, the boys and their sisters played games they made up with cards and dice, and did their school work. While they sat around the kitchen table their mother opened boxes of feathers she'd saved since the summer killings of chickens, geese, and guineas.

"Show your little sister how to do this; it's her first time," their mother said.

"She's too little," Jon complained.

"I'll show her," offered Jane.

"Take a feather, like this." Jon picked one up and tickled her face.

"Don't mind him. Just watch. Strip the center spine off each feather and discard it in this box. Then put the soft feather parts into the big large basket. See? Easy?"

"Why?" the little one asked.

"She always asks 'why' about everything," Jon complained.

"Mother will use the feathers to stuff pillows and comforters. It will keep us warm. There you go, you're doing just fine."

"I'm not too little, Jon," the youngster spouted with her chin in the air. "So there."

Winter was the time for such indoor work, and the farm family chatted amiably near the glowing fire, while working. In the cheery kitchen it was often hard to tell the difference between leisure and work.

One evening after supper, their dad announced he'd brought back a surprise for the family from a trip he'd taken to the city. He carried the wooden crate into the kitchen. He pried the slats loose with a pry bar as his children gathered around excitedly.

"What's in it, Dad?"

"I think it's a chest or a trunk," offered Jon.

"Funny looking trunk," murmured Vytas checking all the sides, peering through the crate's slats.

Vincas had a wide grin on his face. His father looked up at him and winked. Vincas was beside himself, sure that he'd guessed.

Jonas pulled the wooden box out of the crate. He sat the funny looking box on a small table his wife pushed his way. He began tinkering with knobs and dials. Before long, they heard crackling noises coming from the box, followed by a shrill whine. Suddenly a man's voice boomed out of the box. The girls jumped; the boys stared. Vincus grinned. Curious Vytas ventured close and peered around behind it. Their mother scowled, unsure of the safety, and tried to hold him back.

"Get back! Get away from that. It's the devil's mechanism," yelled their grandfather. He was tottering towards them with an axe in his hand.

"I'll take care of it. Move away, Jonas, move away children," he shouted. "That thing is evil. We'll have nothing of the devil's in this house." He raised the axe. His son grabbed his arm from behind.

"No, Tetis. Papa, it's okay. It's fine. We'll put it away." Jonas took the axe from his elderly father and handed it to Vincas who put it back in the firebox. Disappointed, the boys helped their dad put their surprise back into the crate to hide it from their grandfather.

Every evening they waited for their grandfather to retire to his room so Dad could carry out the battery-powered radio and they could listen to stories and music. One evening while listening, they heard a broadcast from Boston, in America, singing Lithuanian songs. Their grandfather came out of his room, grabbed the axe from the firebox and shouted.

"A machination of the devil! Clear that thing out of this house."

"No, Grandpa!" The boys gathered protectively around the radio while their dad intercepted their grandfather.

"Listen, Grandpa. Listen to this." They all began humming along to the familiar tunes. Grandfather knew the words to the traditional folk songs and sang softly, then limply returned to his room.

Not long after, they discovered they could listen to Mass on Sunday, broadcast from the cathedral in Vilnius, the capitol city. When Grandfather crept from his bed and heard the familiar sacred words being chanted from the box he moved toward the radio and dropped to his arthritic knees on the hard floor. Every Sunday after that, he spent that hour kneeling in front of the radio, participating in the far away church service. The family attended church in town whenever they could, but when they were unable, they listened and worshipped with their grandfather kneeling in front of the radio.

Chapter 5

Hunting with the Uncles

Not having many store-bought toys, the boys made their own. They built an arsenal of wooden swords and guns and played war, stalking enemies through the forest or attacking pretend enemies along their school route. They created new card games, while their father read the newspaper, *The Farmers' Advisor*, for advice and farming methods.

"You boys up for hunting this week?" he asked.

"Ja! Ja!" the boys clamored for their favorite pastime. "We want to go, for sure."

"Vytas and I will be the game drivers, Dad," asserted Jon.

Vytas ran to his room and returned with a square of nicely finished wood with grooves routed out on it, and a smooth dowel made from a tree branch in his other hand. He ran the dowel up and down across the grooves creating a melodious zinging sound.

"What do you think? Good, ja?" he handed it to his dad.

"A great noisemaker for game driving," admired his dad. "Nice craftwork, too, Vytas. Ja, you'll be a fine game driver with this noisemaker. And you're getting to be a clever woodworker, too."

"That will sure get the hares running," said Jon excitedly. "I wish wild pigs and wolves weren't so scarce. They'd be a lot more fun than driving hares and foxes."

"But we've a good market for the foxes and hares, Jon. When Trader Jew comes by this month, we'll have a good supply for him. Wolf would be good, too, but I don't think he'd be too keen about pigskin. We've got several nice hares hanging in the granary waiting for him to come. Let's add some more today."

"He's a nice man, isn't he," commented Vytas.

"Yes, and always fair," answered Jonas.

"A good businessman, too, I think. I admire the way he keeps his books," added Vincus. "I might be an accountant someday, too."

"Get ready for hare pie, Mama," Vytas called as they pulled on their boots and coats. She was in the kitchen supervising the two women who helped prepare the meals for the family and four or five farm hands.

"Ja, ja, big talk for a young hunter man," she called back. It was their weekly joke, as her husband generally hunted on Saturdays and his sons always wanted to go.

"Uncles are coming with us today, Dad?" Vincas asked.

"Ja, I think so."

"Good, then we'll have lots of fun," Vytas said. Vytas and Jon glanced at each other and tried not to laugh. They knew if the uncles were along, they'd end up in the forest with the secret brewers, called bootleggers. Vincas gave the boys a quick warning shove and a wink.

Sure enough, when the boys spotted the white smoke puffs above the trees and pointed them out, the uncles decided they needed to check it out, "to be sure it wasn't a forest fire." The boys rolled their eyes at each other and muffled their laughter. They knew, and knew their uncles knew, it was not a forest fire.

The skilled hunters, quiet afoot as usual, surprised the brewers. When the brewers saw the bergenmeister, the top government official in the area, they were nervous. They offered hospitality and everyone, including the boys, got a "shot," a tiny glassful of their illegal brew. After a few drinks the brewers relaxed, realizing the bergenmeister wasn't going to bust up their still or arrest them. After a few more drinks, the hunters left. Their father looked away and ignored the camp.

"Dad, doesn't your job—

"Everyone needs to have a job," he interrupted. "Those men are in violation that's true, but they aren't hurting anyone, and they provide for their families. It's my judgment call. Sometimes a judgment call gets into a puddled area, where it's not all right and not all wrong. I just do the best I can to be fair, and try not to make trouble for folks unnecessarily. We all have enough trouble making a living as it is."

Vytas nodded. "I see."

One such Saturday, after a few drinks, the uncles had difficulty traipsing across the furrows of a plowed field, the favorite hangout of the hares. Stumbling and bumbling, one of the hunters nearly stepped on a hare hidden in the furrow. As the hare jumped up directly in front of him, he tried to step back out of the rut, fell backwards, and the gun went off.

Vytas heard the shot whiz toward him and dove for the dirt as the bullet grazed the sleeve of his sheepskin jacket.

His father was at his side in an instant.

"Are you shot?" he asked breathlessly.

"I'm okay, Dad. I just dodged it. He shouldn't have tried to shoot the hare right in front of him. He could have shot his foot off!"

"Or killed you," his repentant uncle said seriously.

"Really, as close as that hare was, you should have grabbed it by the leg and saved your ammunition," teased Jon.

The careless hunter sat in the dirt. He laid his gun down and dropped his face into his hands.

"I'm so sorry. I think I'll not stop at the brewers while hunting ever again. My judgment...it was impaired...I could have killed my nephew," he wailed.

"I think, Vytas, it would be wise to not mention to your mother that it was almost you who was the hare in the pie today," his dad said.

The boys looked knowingly at each other and the pact was made. What mother doesn't know won't worry her.

Chapter 6

Red Star

Vincus slung his book bag over his shoulder, blew into his chilly hands and shoved them into his coat pocket. Jon and Vytas wrestled, tripped, elbowed, and laughed, fooling around on the path to school. Steamy bursts of their breath cut into the clear, sharp morning air as they hurried along that spring day.

"Haloo," called their cousin Yonas. He was one year older than Vytas. Yonas's mother was their dad's sister. As they passed his farm he joined them on their walk to school. He ran toward them, his worn leather school bag bouncing.

When he reached their group, Vincas scowled at him.

"What is that you are wearing?" Vincus asked gruffly. Jon glared at his cousin, chewed his lip, and clenched his fists. Vytas stared at the red metal star on Yonas' jacket.

Deanna K. Klingel

"I spoke to you, Yonas. What is that pinned on your coat?" The anger rose in Vincus' throat.

"He knows what it is," Vytas growled.

"Looks like a piece of cow dung to me," said Jon.

Vincas grabbed the star and ripped it off Yonas' jacket. He threw it on the ground. "Where cow dung should be," he said loudly.

Vytas stomped on the star, bending, burying, and trampling the hated red symbol.

"Why would you wear such a thing as that?" he spoke angrily at Yonas.

"I don't answer to you," Yonas grumbled. He looked at his trashed star, the symbol of communism, its hammer and sickle now barely recognizable in the dirt.

"I'll report you. I will. You'll be sorry you did that." Yonas fought back his tears.

"You don't believe in communism. How could you? You're too smart to fall for its lies," Vytas said, scuffing the dirt in the direction of the star, burying it further.

"It's not lies. I'm going to report you, and you'll change your tune," Yonas shot back angrily.

Vincas snatched cousin Yonas by the collar. Vytas grabbed Yonas's arms and held them at his back. They stood nose-to-nose, toe-to-toe.

"You'll have a lot of explaining to do to the family if you do, Yonas," Vincus snarled. They shoved their cousin ahead of them. Yonas looked over his shoulder and began jogging to stay ahead of his three angry cousins.

The boys were unnerved and the school day dragged. They all wanted to talk to their father. They ran most of the way home in the semi-darkness at four o'clock.

"So, that's how it happened, Dad," Vytas explained after supper. Their father laid his broad, callused hands on the boys' shoulders.

"I know why you did that. I don't fault you. I probably would have done the same, and I would have been as angry as you. I'm shamed for my nephew. But, we must be careful. I've always had suspicions about Yonas's father. My brother-in-law distances himself from the family, and I've noticed his leftist ideals. I've had suspicions. I don't know what my sister knows. Whether Yonas really believes in communism or just playing along, we can't be sure. But, I think his father may. So, we must be careful, boys."

"Yes, Dad," they all agreed. "We understand."

Danute 1930s

Chapter 7

Getting Even

All was quiet this evening in the usually bustling city of Kaunas, the second largest city in Lithuania. The lace curtains at the open window fluttered lightly and Danute sat up in her bed. She'd not been asleep, just twilight dreaming, waiting for the quiet to settle around her and the moon to light her room. *My moon,* she thought. *It's shining just for me and keeping my secrets.* Her bare feet tiptoed across the carpet in the third story of the brick apartment building. With practiced silence, she removed a book from her shelf. Quieter than a mouse, she slid back into bed, opened the book and rested it on her propped knees in the beam of the moonlight.

"You look tired this morning, Danute, did you not sleep well last night?" asked Sofyia in the morning. "It is already late and your brothers are already out and about. It will be good when summer ends and you go back to school. This is a lazy hour, not fitting for a lady."

Danute shrugged and ate her breakfast. Sofyia their maid might be a nag, but she made the best breakfast. Danute ate her pancakes and veal sausages. Sofyia cooked, cleaned, organized the house and looked after Danute and her brothers and littler sister.

"Where's Mama?" Danute asked.

"She's at her ladies club meeting. I don't know anything more. Eat. I need to clean up. You are making me late with your laziness."

Danute ate, excused herself, and went to her room. Opening the large wardrobe doors she studied her clothes, clean, pressed, hanging with all the accessories organized for wearing. She imagined picking out a dress from here, a pinafore from over there, and wearing any collar or cuff she chose. *But, no. That won't do. Mother leaves the orders and Sofyia carries them out. Someday I will make up my own rules. I'll dress however I please and go wherever I want and be with anyone I choose.* For now she would have to be content to choose from the summer play dresses Sofyia organized for her in the wardrobe. When school started, she wouldn't be able to choose even that. She would be wearing her brown school uniform dress covered with a pinafore, white collar, white cuffs, apron, and brown shoes. *Dull*, she sighed with resignation. *Dull, dull, dull.*

"Bring your hairbrush, Danute. Snap it up," called Sofyia. Danute bounced down the stairs and tried to stand still while Sofyia brushed and twisted her long blonde hair into two braids that she criss-crossed and pinned on the back of the wiggling girl's head.

"This hair will be down before dinner," Sofyia predicted. "Now shoo. Go play. And your mother said 'don't get dirty.'"

Of course she did, thought Danute. *She says that every day.* With her book and a doll she headed out the front door of their three-story apartment building, into her world. She knew most of the neighbors, mostly professional people, or army. Most of the adults came and went mysteriously as her own parents did, while the maids enforced family rules.

She didn't know many of the grownups, except to know which building they lived in, but she was familiar with all the maids who refereed, slapped sense into them, provided treats for tea parties and got them to daily Mass on time. The maids kept them safe, clean, and fed, held them to their family rules and managed to instill courtesy, honesty, and self-reliance. The maids were feared, but respected and loved in their proxy-parent roles.

Danute sat on the front steps, her back against the railing, and opened the book she'd been reading last night in the moonlight.

"Ouch!" she shrieked and jumped to her feet. Before she could stand and turn around, the giggling boy dashed around the corner of the building.

"You better think twice before you pinch me again, Victor. You're going to be sorry!" Hands on her hips, lips in a serious pout, Danute began to plan revenge.

"Want to play house with our dolls?" asked the neighbor girl from her own steps. "You can come over, or I'll come there." Danute looked down at her doll flopped on the porch on her china face. She loved to play house with her dolls, but usually played alone. Now she wondered if she might be getting too grown to play dolls. Besides, her mother didn't like her to associate with other kids in the neighborhood, believing them to be "unsuitable" companions. Danute preferred reading alone anyway, so she answered, "Not today. I've got a headache." That wasn't totally untruthful. Her brother Victor was her headache.

The neighbor skipped down her steps and headed off in another direction, her doll cradled in her arms. Danute rubbed the smarting bruise on the back of her arm, frowned, and planned her revenge. She hunched into the corner and resumed her tactical planning. Before long she quietly opened the front door and slipped unnoticed up the stairs to her room.

She filled a small bathing basin with water and carried it to her open window, balancing it precariously. *Why is water so heavy, I wonder? It doesn't look heavy.*

She ducked behind the curtain and window frame where she could watch the front steps without being seen. She heard them before she saw them. There he was, her brother Victor; mouthy, bossy Victor. He was one year younger than her, and he acted like an old czar. He was such a pest. And now she'd get even.

Victor waved to his friends who continued down the street. He took his ball and jacks from his pocket. She watched and she waited. When he finished playing he put the ball and jacks into his pocket and leaned back on the steps. Balanced on his elbows, he stretched out his legs, and looked into the summer sky, totally relaxed, eyes closed, mouth opened.

Danute pushed the tub forward on the sill just a bit. She held tightly to the handle with one hand and with the other she jerked the tub downwards.

Hit with the deluge of cold water, Victor hopped about in a rage.

"Hey!" he shouted, "Who did that? Danute, you'll be sorry!" He leaped off the steps howling, choking, and spitting. Danute pulled the tub inside and dropped beneath the window collapsing in laughter. She could hear Victor spouting in the street below. When she heard the front door slam, she shoved the basin under the bed and crawled into her wardrobe pulling the door closed behind her. She had a little string attached to the inside of the door for just such an occasion; it had proved handy many times. Victor was banging on her bedroom door.

"Let me in! You'll pay for this." He flung the door open and charged in. Met with silence in the tidy empty room, he could think of nothing more to say.

Sofyia tromped up the stairs behind him. "You get out the house with this water. You are making puddles on the stairs. You brought water everywhere. More trouble than the dogs," she yelled. She grabbed Victor by the ear and shoved him into the hall with a rapid stream of instructions about cleaning up the mess.

"It's her fault," he accused. "Danute did this. Make her clean it up."

"Danute is playing dolls with the neighbor girl. You don't sass me or your mother will hear of it. Get this mopped up now. You'll wash your own clothes and hang them outside. Get to it, snap snap."

Danute wiggled into the corner of the wardrobe, getting comfortable and giggling to herself. She snapped on her penlight and opened her book.

Chapter 8

Independent Girl

Danute, born in 1930, had started school at age 6. No one was sure when she really started reading; no one could remember when she couldn't read. Even though her parents didn't involve themselves much in their four children's upbringing, they were consistent with their evening ritual of family reading. Every evening after supper the family gathered and a member of the family would read aloud to the others. Perhaps it was her desire to be part of this ritual that encouraged Danute to learn to read at such an early age.

The nuns at her school were impressed with her reading ability. They weren't so impressed with her tree-climbing talent. Along with Danute's mother, they set out to reform the skinny tomboy and set her on a righteous path suitable for a lady before she beat up every boy in her class.

It wasn't that she didn't want to be a lady. She loved dressing up in fine clothes and entertaining. She determined early on she would be an independent woman, and not be a servant to any husband. Danute wasn't particularly close to her mother. She didn't spend a lot of time with her, but she admired her mother's independence and stature among the women of the neighborhood.

"I'll come and go and do as I please, just like Mother," she told everyone. Danute adored her father. Because he was in the military, he was often away from home. He doted on his daughter and returned from every trip bearing another doll for her huge collection. He took her on special dinner dates to fancy restaurants where she could wear pretty shoes and carry her little purse.

She took advantage of her many hours alone to visit her mother's room and try on her high-heeled shoes, clomping across the floor. Danute liked the sound of ladies' heels clicking on the floor. It was while trying on her mother's many pair of shoes, she happened to discover the portable Singer Sewing Machine stored in her mother's wardrobe.

Always interested in everything mechanical, Danute wanted to know how it worked. She unfastened the cover, lifted it off, and beheld a beautiful, shiny machine with many tiny moveable parts. She turned the wheel, lifted the levers, unscrewed little screws and screwed them back in. She moved the presser foot up and down. She just had to learn to sew! She decided she'd be a clothing designer when she grew up; she knew it was her destiny. How could she learn? Who could show her? If she got caught with the machine she would be standing in the corner...again.

Danute spent many hours standing in the corner, punishment for everything from disobedience, sauciness, getting dirty, tardiness or a bad report from school. It wouldn't be so bad if she could have a book with her in the corner, but no, it was total: no talking, no moving, no eyes looking, no reading. *What about sewing? Maybe sewing could be my punishment. I could beg, "Please don't make me sew while I'm standing in the corner!" I could make my dolls some new dresses out of Mama's scraps.*

She dreamed the pretty dress she could sew for herself for her mother's next dinner party. Their family entertained a good deal. Easter and Christmas were the favorite times for Danute and her brothers because other children were more likely to accompany the dinner guests. Even though children were seen and not heard at table, she loved the excitement and dressing up. It wasn't her fault her clothes were a mess before the first guest arrived; things just seemed to happen to her nice clothes.

The dining room table was always set as if company was expected any moment. The long linen tablecloths, intricately embroidered with Lithuanian designs, were spread beneath the gleaming candlesticks and crystal goblets. A banquet could be produced at the wave of Mama's magic hand, Danute believed.

"Will we put the little paper hats on the lamb?" Danute asked Sofyia. "I want to help."

"You are in my way. But, ah, there you are. You must learn. Here. Do it this way."

"I know how to do it," Danute declared. After all, she saw it done all the time. She mashed the little papers into the juicy meat, and Sofyia threw her hands into the air in desperation.

"Why don't you go with your brothers and gather table decorations from the forest, heh? We'll make a nice centerpiece. Go, shoo. Snap snap."

Danute ran after her brothers, who were determined to outrun her and leave her crying alone in the street. *They think I'm a cry baby. They'll see.* She took a quick ninety degree turn into the deep woods at the end of the block, a short cut, running for all she was worth. Her pinafore tore on blackberry bushes. Her shoe slid into a wet spring, but she ran on, kicking mud onto the tail of her dress. When she got to the foot bridge where they gathered mushrooms for the gravy and mosses for the table decoration, she sat down and took a deep breath to regain her composure. She smoothed her dress and tried to look as if she'd been there all day. She heard branches cracking beneath the running boys' feet. She looked up coyly, as if surprised.

"Oh, there you are," she said casually. "I was afraid you were lost."

"How did—

"Where—did you—

The boys bent over panting, hands on their thighs catching their breath.

"Well, let's get gathering," she said, trying not to smile. She carefully laid the mosses and other pretty things from the woods on the tray Sofyia had sent with the boys. Her brothers pulled mushrooms from the damp bank and dropped them into the mesh bag for Sofyia's gravy.

"Good girl," Sofyia said curtly as Danute handed her the tray of mosses for the table centerpiece. "Now get yourself dressed. Quickly now, snap snap."

The table was set, as always, with the best china and Czechoslovakian crystal. Silver candlesticks and gleaming candles lit the room. Sweet liqueurs in tiny crystal cups projected rainbows reflecting on the tablecloth that fascinated Danute. Herrings and eggs nestled on silver platters, and vinegretas, an assortment of vegetable side dishes, in small crystal dishes would be offered to guests with the first course, followed by twelve main dishes.

Christmas Eve was the only celebration that didn't include meat, only fish dishes. But, Christmas Day they enjoyed plenty of meat, and they always had ham at Easter, presented artistically on silver platters.

Danute scooted up the stairs to her room, threw open the wardrobe door and perused her well-organized clothes. She knew in which section her dinner clothes hung. Would anyone notice if she wore something other than velvet? Certainly no one would notice if she didn't wear a stiffly starched collar. *No one will look at me at dinner, not really. I want to choose for myself.* She took her favorite dress off the hanger. This cotton dress was comfortable and only had one hook at the neck, front and back. In fact, she thought it looked the same either way, front or back, didn't matter. She tossed it over her head, slipped on her nice shoes and put a flower in her braids. She licked her hand and slicked back the straggling hair hanging by her face. She thought she looked pretty good. Best of all, she wasn't late, so Sofyia wouldn't be upset with her.

Chapter 9

Dinner Party

No one was in the dining room. She walked around the large table admiring how pretty it looked. She thought she could improve on the mosses, wildflowers, and acorns in the centerpiece. She squeezed between the chairs and leaned in, picking up pieces of the centerpiece, trying them in different ways, rearranging until she was sure they looked better. Dirt dropped onto the tablecloth. She picked up one of the white linen napkins and brushed the dirt onto the carpet. Shaking the soiled napkin, she turned it upside down, and laid it back on the table over the smudge. She wiped her dirty hands down the front of her dress. Everything looked just fine, she thought.

As she was leaving the room, she noticed the new brass candle lighter-snuffer-wick trimmer combination tool on the side table. Danute's curiosity for all things mechanical drew her to it. She was fascinated by its moving parts and wondered how it worked exactly. She began to putter with it, twisting, pushing, scissoring, and pulling the small brass parts. She thought she'd almost figured out how it worked, when she heard Sofyia's heavy shoes rapidly approaching. Startled, she dropped the gadget immediately. It splashed into the punch bowl. The deep burgundy liquid trickled down the front of her dress. She stood at attention as Sofyia hustled in and out of the room with bread trays, barely noticing Danute. Then, she stopped at the doorway and turned.

"Danute? What you doing here?"

"Just looking at how pretty the table looks. That's all. Nothing else." She managed an angelic smile.

"Good. Go on now. Shoo. Out. Snap snap."

Danute folded her hands obediently and marched out of the room. Sofyia hustled past her leaving a breeze in her wake; Danute scurried out of her way. When she saw herself in the hall mirror she gasped. Sofyia had been too busy to notice, but Danute was in big trouble. The black soil finger prints and the stream of burgundy screamed trouble!

The doorbell chimed; the guests were arriving. Quickly she peeled her arms out of the stained and smudged dress, turned it around, front to back, put her arms back in and backed against the wall. Sofyia answered the door.

"Danute, take the guests' wraps, carry them to the bedroom, and then announce the guests to your mother." Danute moved sideways towards the guests, her back against the wall, smiled, took their wraps and walked backwards down the hall to the bedroom where she deposited the coats. The guests looked oddly at her, glanced at each other and shrugged.

"It's the age," one woman whispered.

When called to dine, Danute sidled into the dining room, back against the wall, and crab walked to her chair. Her mother stared. She studied the cotton dress and glowered. Danute smiled sweetly at everyone around the table and bowed her head for the blessing. She sat straight and firm with the dirty, stained dress hidden against the chair back, and politely passed the bread.

Just as dessert torte was offered, Danute covered a feigned yawn, and rubbed her eyes.

"May I be excused, please, Mother." Her mother scowled at her, but nodded. Danute stood, backed up, and walked backwards out of the room. Once she was away from the dining room, she ran up the stairs to her room, slipped out of her dress and hid it under the mattress. She tossed her nightgown over her head and climbed into bed with her book and pen light, prepared to be asleep if anyone should come looking for her.

When her father came in the morning, Danute tried to look ill, hoping he'd take pity on her.

"Danute, were you ill at dinner last evening? Are you feeling okay today?"

"Ja, Father, much better."

"That's good. Come here. We have something to talk about."

Uh oh. Danute could tell by his tone he was serious. She thought she was in deep trouble. She gulped. When he saw the distressed look on her face, he wrapped his arm around her.

"You aren't in trouble, little one. No, not you. It's something else. You see, we have to move. We need to leave Kaunus."

"But, why? This is our place."

"It is. But, we can make another home, in another place. It will be fine, you'll see. There are things going on around us, Danute. Unpleasant things. Some people think it could even lead to war. People are disappearing, and others are forced to move. I think it is best if we move because we *choose* to move, don't you?"

"Well, I guess so."

"You tell too much," scolded her mother. "Danute is seven. She is too young to understand. My own father was killed in the Russian Revolution. God rest his soul." She crossed herself. "My mother raised us children alone. You can't understand what that was like. Children should be spared from such nightmares." Danute watched her mother wipe her eyes with her pretty handkerchief, then hastily leave the room.

"I'm not too young, Father. I understand." Danute jumped off the bed and began pulling her stockings and underwear out of the bureau.

"I'll get packed," she said. "I understand. Where are we going to go? What will be our new place? Where will we go to school?"

"We're going to Simkaiciai. We'll be closer to our relatives there. You'll like that, won't you? I think that will be safer for now, than the city."

"Yes, aunts and uncles. I understand. I do." She stuffed her socks and underwear into a small satchel along with a doll and a book.

Chapter 10

Country Bees

Later that summer, after the family had resettled in Simkaiciai, the three youngest children, Danute, Victor, and their younger sister Ilona, were sent to visit relatives for a while. The relatives had no children and lived on a large plantation. They had many workers, but Danute's father thought it would be a good experience for his city children, and suggested they be given some jobs so they could learn some useful skills.

After only a few hours, Danute, Ilona, and Victor decided farm work wasn't for them and they set out to investigate the place. They walked around the barns, gardens, and fields, complaining of the stench and bugs.

"I hate the country," said Danute. "There's nothing to do here. It smells. I miss the city."

"Me, too. I want to go to our new place in Simky-whatever it's called," pouted Ilona.

When they came upon a row of small wooden houses, whitewashed with tiny windows, Danute ran towards them thinking they looked like a little village of doll houses.

"What a sweet little toy village," she exclaimed. "Look, Ilona. Isn't it pretty?"

"What can they be for?" Victor wondered. Danute knelt close and peered into a tiny window.

"There's bugs in there! I don't think they intend flies and bugs to be in this little house. We should fix that. We're supposed to do work; let's clean house."

"Here," said Victor. He handed small sticks to Danute and Ilona, and demonstrated with his own stick how to rid the little house of bugs. They ran their sticks across the little windows and poked the sticks inside. Within seconds, the resident honey bees unleashed a fury like the city children had never seen. With the black swarm streaming after them, they ran screaming to the house.

Still sobbing and hiccupping, the three children, covered in welts, lay huddled on a sofa while kitchen workers grated heaps of carrots into a soft mash and applied it to their stings.

Danute thought she'd learned as much about farming as she ever cared to know.

"I just want the summer to end so we can get back to the city, back to our new place in Simkaiciai, and back to school. Then all we have to fear is Russian soldiers, no bees."

Chapter 11

Icy River

Winter was truly Danute's favorite time of year. The long dark hours were anything but dreary for a reader of books. She loved winter: the thick wooly coats and mittens and hot food for supper, kugalish and zeppelins with meat inside topped with sour cream, sledding, snow, and card games. But most of all, lots of hours spent reading her books by the fire in their new place.

"Come on," her older brother Kent said one frosty Sunday afternoon. "Get dressed. We're all going out."

"I don't want to go. I want to read." Danute admired Kent, four years older than her, because he was almost grown and could do what he pleased. But, she resented him telling her what to do.

"Danute, come on. You can read later, after it gets dark. You can't see the beauty of the snow in the dark or with your nose in a book. I want to show you something. Before long the snow will be gone and you won't have seen it. Don't I always show you good things? Come on. I'm older, do as I say."

"I'll come, but not because *you* said so. Because *I* decided," she said. They piled on their coats, scarves, hats, and mittens and followed Kent. The street was slushy and the sun was peeking out from fluffy clouds, warm and shining. It did seem as if winter was trying to say goodbye. Perhaps spring came early here in Simikaiciai. They heard the drip, drop of the melt on the roofs. Stomping their boots, they squirted gray slush at each other. They followed Kent to the Naminous River which flowed through the town in the summer. In the winter the river lay frozen and silver, completely silent. Today, it couldn't decide. Part of the frozen river was beginning to move. The ice looked wet and shiny. It looked like a jigsaw puzzle falling apart one piece at a time.

"Come on," called Kent. He leaped off the snowy bank onto a large ice floe that hadn't yet unlocked. He began hopping from floe to floe. Occasionally one would teeter and he caught his balance like an agile circus performer. Victor and Danute laughed. Victor, not to be outdone, hopped out onto a floe and did a little jig, causing the floe to split in half and getting his foot wet. The three laughed and laughed. Kent struck a pose.

"I'm a snow sculpture," he shouted. "Come on, Danute. Don't be a scaredy girl!"

"She probably can't do this. Girls can't do this kind of thing," said Victor.

"Girls can do anything boys can do, Victor" she retorted. She hopped off the bank to a floe. Her foot slipped and she fell down onto the sheet of ice. As it broke away, it tilted toward the side where she lay. Danute rolled off into the water, screaming.

"Here, take my hand," yelled Victor. When he leaned over to grasp her coat sleeve, the floe he was on flipped into the air. Victor plunged into the icy river. Danute screamed and thrashed about in the water. Her heavy wool coat was soaked and was soon heavy as an anchor. Kent hopped from floe to floe cracking, chipping, and breaking them as he went. Just as he reached his brother and sister the entire ice mass cracked with a loud bang that echoed up and down the bank like gunshots. The river roared its release from winter's captivity and commenced it's wildly raging flow. Broken sheets of ice flew past them and shot dangerously over the currents. Kent grabbed Danute's coat.

"Victor, swim," he shouted over the roar of the freshening river. "Watch the floes, they'll decapitate you!" Danute, who didn't know how to swim, was terrified. She panicked as her heavy coat weighed her down and huge chunks of ice flew past her, their sharp edges slicing through the water and cutting the ice in its way. She splashed frantically but the weight of her coat pulled her under the water just as a huge sharp chunk of ice whooshed over her head. She was so cold she hardly cared that her hair was pulling painfully.

Victor was the first on the shore dragging his sister by her hair. She and Kent crawled breathlessly onto the shore, shaking and shivering, unable to speak.

"We have to move," commanded Victor. "If we stand still, we'll freeze to death, and Mama will be angry. Run for home. Run as fast as you can to stay warm."

Kent, for the moment, seemed too stunned to do anything, too overwhelmed by his responsibility. "What have I done?" His whispered voice froze in the frost gathering about his face.

"I hate you!" screamed Danute. Kent shoved her hard to get her moving. Victor grabbed her hand and dragged her along. They ran along on wooden legs with knees and ankles too cold to bend. The three arrived home with a coating of hoary frost covering them, out of breath, and blue with cold, their clothing frozen stiff. They all held frozen hands.

"If we didn't have bad enough luck," mumbled Kent, "I think Mother is at home." The three gulped and prepared themselves for a fury equal to the Naminous River.

"I don't know whether to spank you or call the doctor," their mother exploded. She paced up and down the hallway, back and forth.

"What gets into your heads? How could you do this? Have you not the sense you were born with? You surely try my patience. Whose idea was this? Never mind. Oh my, my... oh, Sofyia, take care of them, before I kill them." She stormed away.

"Get into the tub," demanded Sofyia. "When you are warm you will take care of this mess of clothes. You could have died, you know. Jesus, Mary, and Joseph, Saints preserve us," she huffed.

"I'm not getting in the tub with *them*." Danute glared at her brothers. "I'm going to wait by the fire."

"Suit yourself then," Sofyia said sharply. "You always do."

Danute wrapped herself in a blanket, and sat down pouting and shivering in front of the fireplace. Her frozen hair began to thaw and the cold water dripped down her cheeks. Her hands were shaking, her insides quaked. She just wanted to be alone.

"Thank you, God, I'm not drowned," she prayed. "Mother Mary, I'm sorry. I don't mean to be bad. I want to be as good as your Son I'm just not so good at it. Things just happen. Thank you, Jesus, for saving me. I didn't know you could swim."

Lithuania's Children 1939

Lithuania's Children

For the children of Lithuania, Name Day is an important day, as the Birthday is in America. In 1939, when Vytas and Danute were nine years old, and Danute was having her name day, Germany demanded Lithuania surrender her seaport or face a full Nazi invasion. Lithuania and the other small Baltic countries had been able to play Germany and Russia against each other, but in March 1939, Adolph Hitler arrived in the coastal port city of Klaipeda and claimed it for Germany.

In August, Russia's Joseph Stalin and Germany's Hitler signed the Nazi-Soviet Pact and began to divide Eastern Europe between them, as if it all belonged to them. Russia occupied Lithuania in 1940. Mass deportations to Siberia began. Friends, neighbors, and relatives disappeared in the terror of the dark Baltic nights at the hands of ruthless Russians.

Fear thickened like a fog over the country sides and over the cities. Lithuanians hid and moved at night.

Hitler wasn't satisfied. In a ploy for Lithuania's cooperation, Germany let the nation know Germany would protect them from Russian domination. They would be a good neighbor and ally. In 1941, Nazi Germany began to occupy Russia's Lithuania. Lithuanians trekked toward Prussia, the German border, to stay ahead of the Russian defense, and looked to Germany for protection.

DANUTE 1939

Chapter 12

Name Day

Relatives and guests arrived for Danute's ninth name day.

Today should be a happy day. Why is everyone so glum? Her favorite meal and the beautiful centerpiece she'd helped Sofyia make with pebbles and wildflowers wasn't being noticed or commented on. The grownups passed those looks with their eyes, thinking children don't notice. But, Danute did notice. She noticed the grownups were wiggling in their chairs, as if trying to get comfortable. They cleared their throats to speak, then shut their mouths without saying anything. Her uncle secretly pulled the lace curtain back slightly so he could peer unnoticed into the street; Danute noticed. The women talked softly, shook their heads, twisted their Damask napkins nervously, and clucked their tongues.

There was no real conversation, not the happy chatter and clinking of glasses that usually took place around a festive table at a name day. At the end of the evening, the farewells lingered longer than usual, softer, quieter, as if parting was difficult.

They act like they aren't going to see each other again, Danute thought. *I wonder what's going on?* When she tucked into her nightgown, she ventured to ask.

"Mama, what is everyone worrying over? Is it something bad?"

"It's not for children to be worrying about. It's not right that children should worry. Go to sleep. Say your prayers then go to sleep." Her mother was hurrying out of the room just as her father stepped in. They paused in the doorway and looked at each other. Ilona ran across the hall and jumped onto Danute's bed beside her.

"Yes, little ones. Something bad has happened." He looked at his wife. "The children must be informed, or they can't be held in safety. They must all be told. I think Kent has learned of it already. I will go to Victor next."

Their mother crossed herself, put her hands over her face, burst into tears, and hurried out of the room.

"What is it Father? Will you tell it to me and Ilona?" He embraced the girls. Danute pressed her head against his shoulder. She nestled in his arms even as her stomach tightened in fear of what she was going to hear.

"It's the Russians, my daughters. They have taken over Lithuania."

"Are we Russians now?" Ilona asked, wide-eyed.

"No!" He jumped up and stood tall and straight. "No. We are Lithuanians. We will never be Russian. We are Lithuanians forever. Never forget that."

"What is it then? What do the Russians do?" asked Danute.

"They've confiscated everything we have. They've taken my pension from the army. Everything we own is now theirs. We will have a tough time for a while. Our relatives will support us and see us through until I can go back to being a pharmacist. I was a good pharmacist, too, before I became a soldier. It will be all right."

Danute could tell by his scowl he didn't really believe that. *Grownups always pretend.*

"You can work at the drugstore on the corner," offered Ilona brightly.

"No. Thank you, but no. I must keep a low profile for now. Our family is on a list to be sent to Siberia. Since I'm considered just an army official I'm not really a priority. They will be satisfied with merely starving me. But, I mustn't come to their attention."

Danute shivered inside her abdomen and squeezed Ilona's hand.

"We won't starve, Father. I'm learning to cook. Sofyia is teaching me. I'll feed us," brave Ilona said. Her father smiled at his daughters.

"I guess if your dolls can eat mud pies and drink rain water tea, we can too. A strange lesson in humility..."

Danute scowled and twisted her worried mouth. "Siberia is a long way. We have it on a map at school. Why do the Russian soldiers want us to go there?"

"Russia collects people—lots of people— thousands of people--Lithuanians, Belarusians, Latvians, Estonians, Ukrainians, from all the small Baltic countries, to be free laborers for their factories and their forests. They work the people as their slaves until they die."

"That's shameful, Father. Someone should make them stop." Danute crossed her arms indignantly and pursed her lips.

"Perhaps the Germans will come to help us make them stop, as they have promised. Pray for that. Good night, my darling daughters. Sleep now. Come, Ilona, I'll tuck you in. Then I must visit Victor's room."

Chapter 13

Nora and Bopka

Though Danute preferred to be alone with her dolls, books, and her thoughts, she welcomed Nora and Bopka whenever they appeared. Nora, the family's large, noble German Shepherd, was the envy of the neighborhood. Everyone supposed she was the family's security, though the family rather doubted the sweet-natured dog was much of a guard dog. Bopka, a beautiful little dog with lots of hair and bushy tail, was adored by everyone. Though the dogs didn't sleep with the children, both dogs knew the whereabouts of every family member at any moment in time.

Nora barked and ran to the door. Sofyia heard the loud commotion in the street.

"What is that ruckus? What are the neighborhood children up to now?" She hurried to the door. Kent rushed to her side.

"I'm not sure you should open it. I think the Russians are making some trouble," whispered Kent. Sofyia cracked the door slightly ajar to peer out and see what the yelling and hollering were about. Nora snarled, barked, and pried her way through Sofyia's legs, pushed the door ajar, and leaped out on the street. The Russians were running and shouting, and firing their guns in the air. Nora ran around the apartment building, barking. Russian soldiers chased behind her.

"Dogs are not allowed!" they shouted.

"Kill all the dogs!" Gunshots blasted off the apartment buildings. Windows shattered. Bricks splintered. Nora disappeared. Sofyia slammed the door and with her back solidly against it, and refused the children.

"You cannot go out. You'll be shot, too. Too much confusion in the street. No, you cannot go out."

"But Nora needs us," pleaded Danute.

"She's dead!" shouted Victor angrily. "They shot her." He was making a giant effort not to cry. Danute sobbed loudly.

"Nora, Nora," sniffed Ilona. "Our sweet Nora. Oh, God, please send dog angels to watch over Nora."

"We have to go to her. Please, Sofyia. The Russians won't hurt us. We have to find Nora."

"No, Sofyia is right, Danute. We can't go out. The Russians...don't cry, now. It will be okay." Kent lived a private life, and was sometimes bossy, but sometimes, like now, Danute actually liked her older brother.

"How can it be okay? It's Nora, Kent, our Nora." He touched her tenderly.

"I know. She's our special dog." Uncontrolled tears ran silently down the eldest boy's cheeks.

"Can we make a novena for her, Kent?"

The next day during the quiet of the afternoon, Sofyia heard scratching on the door.

"Look who's here!" she shouted. The children came running and the lame dog danced merrily around them all while they hugged and petted their beloved Nora. They washed the dried blood from her flank, cleaned her wound, and bound it up. They gave her meat, and doted on her. Bopka was happy to see her playmate back home, too. She whined a little song and pranced circles around her companion. Her tail waved merrily.

When their father came home after a few days, the excited children told him what had happened while he'd been away.

"If the Russians said no dogs can be here, we cannot risk it. They are only looking for excuses to hurt us in any way, to catch us out on some trifle. It isn't safe for Nora to stay here, not for Nora, or for us. I will make some arrangements."

The children begged, pleaded, and cried. Even his darling daughter exclaiming she hated him and would never speak to him again, couldn't prevail on him to change his mind. He brought home a forest ranger who he had known for many years.

"With a forest ranger is a good place for Nora to live. He's kind to animals and he needs a companion for his lonely life. This is all good, you will see. Nora will be safe then, and well cared for. She'll be in the forest and the Russians will not see her." The children weren't convinced. Danute stormed out of the room, determined to never speak to her father again.

Nora, looking over her shoulder with puzzled eyes, left on the end of a rope with the forest ranger. The silent, sad children slumped on the steps. A couple days later supper was interrupted by scratching at the door.

"Guess who's here?" Sofyia called again. Supper was all but forgotten. The homecoming celebration was short-lived, however. The forest ranger came and took Nora away again. It was another sad moment for the children.

VYTAS 1941-44

Chapter 14

Young Patriot

He flung the shuttered doors open in the second story of the grain barn. He stretched his lanky twelve year-old body to its full measure and inhaled the glorious autumn air.

"The Baltic sky looks deep as an ocean," he called to his cousin Robert in the wagon below.

"Dreamer," Robert answered. "Better get back to work before your father catches you lolling about. Uncle Jonas expects us to finish this."

"Not a dreamer," Vitas shouted. "I'm not a dreamer, I'm a patriot. I'm a Lithuanian patriot."

His two brothers working beside him dropped their grain shovels. One tackled Vytas, the other yanked the rope slamming the shutter doors closed.

The cousin in the wagon leaped to the ground and clambered up the loft ladder. The boys wrestled on the grain-covered floor.

"What are you saying?" hissed Vincas. "Do you want to get us all shot?" He shook Vitas angrily. "You should know better. Even Jon knows better."

"We should fill your mouth with barley. You must keep your thoughts to yourself," spouted Robert, the son of their father's brother.

"Why do you not feel the danger? Are you careless or stupid?" growled Jon.

"All right, all right, get off me," Vytas pleaded.

"Don't ever say that word aloud again, Vytas, for all our sakes. One careless word and our entire family gets hauled off to Siberia." Vincas said.

The other boys stood up and brushed the barley off their shorts.

"You go back to work. I want to have a word with Vytas. Dad will return soon, so all of you go down to the wagon." Jon and Robert descended the ladder while Vincas and Vytas sat on the floor. Vytas hugged his knees as anger flushed his face. He slapped the grain out of his hair.

"Vytas, I know how you feel. Our lives are not turning out how we thought. Everything is wrong. But, there's nothing we can—"

"Yes, there is something we can do. We are all Lithuanians. We live in a free country. The Russians have no right to any of it. We have to get them out of our country. We should all stand up here and yell all the way to the sea, 'I am Lithuanian. I am free. I am a patriot.'"

Vincas grabbed Vytas's shoulders and shook him. "And for that bit of patriotism you and our family will die. Listen, Vytas, everyone feels the way you do. The Russians are destroying us. First it's our economy. They take all our industry, our machinery, and haul them to Russia. They take away our jobs. They make us dependent on them. Now they take our prosperous farms and make them into collectives that collapse as we watch. Then we have no food. We must let their government feed us. Our people are herded like cattle into rail cars and never heard from again. Soon there will be no Lithuania. Lithuanians will all be gone." His voice dropped to a whisper.

"Then what difference does it make? We will all die anyway. We should die as patriots."

"Our only hope is to live, Vytas, don't you see? As long as we're alive we can hope. The Germans are coming; they'll get the Russians out. They will save us. The Germans are coming to free us, but we have to be alive if we're to be saved. You want to be a patriot? Then start by saving your family. Keep your mouth shut."

"Ja. I will do it." Vytas grudgingly accepted the cuff on his shoulder from his older brother.

"See here, Vytas," Vincas reopened the loft doors and pointed out. "As far as you can see- farm land. Good farm land. Going wasted because of Russia's ignorance. Last night, another family… gone, just like that." Vincas snapped his fingers and Vytas stared at him.

"The whole family? Gone? How do whole families just vanish, Vincus? Where do they go? What's to be done? Who will watch their farm and their stock?"

"Like all the others. All of us will help. Family members will come and see to it."

"Then they, too, disappear in the night. Do you think we might be next, Vincas?" Vytas shuddered. His boyish bravado and joking good nature usually overrode any fear of being arrested and hauled off, disappearing from the farm, the community, his family. But, he recognized this shudder. It was fear.

"So what do we do, then? We just wait here? We harvest for *them,* and then they come harvest us?"

"Ja, maybe so."

Chapter 15

Tragic Shot

Vytas woke to hear arguing outside. It was his father and an uncle. The sun was barely up. The roosters crowed. Vytas peered out from behind the lace curtain.

"I want you to come, too. The time is now. Germans are showing up in other towns. The Russians are leaving our town. It is time to take it back. Now!" His uncle was upset.

"It is too early. There are still Russians in the forests, lurking everywhere. We must be patient." His father paced and gestured.

"It's not like you to shirk, Jonas."

"I'm not shirking, I'm thinking. You are not. You're being hasty. It's too early to do this. You're a sergeant in the army, you should have better sense. We have to have patience, man. You're just being hot-headed now and it will cost you. No, I'll not be part of this plan at this time. Later, maybe."

When the argument was over, Vytas watched his father pedal his bicycle alongside his uncle and another man. They were heading toward town.

The three boys gathered for breakfast, then clustered about the farmyard organizing their morning chores.

"Did you hear them? Did you hear them arguing this morning?" Vytas asked.

Vincus nodded. Jon shook his head.

"What were they arguing about?" he asked. Vincus and Vytas shared a glance. They shrugged as if they didn't know.

Later their father returned, alone, shaken, and pale. His wife sat him down and gave him broth. The boys lurked quietly outside the open kitchen window.

"Tell me what has happened," she said fearfully, stroking her husband's brow.

"We had only gone half way to the town. I should have stopped him. I tried, but, he wouldn't listen. He was being so hot-headed. I told him there were Russians all around, hiding in the forest, but he didn't want to believe me. He insisted the Germans in town had scared them all away. But there they were, right in front of us. Seven Russians on horseback in the field ahead of us, and the three of us on bicycles. I told him, 'Stop now,' I said to him, 'while there is still time.' But he wouldn't stop. He pedaled straight at them. I couldn't believe he could be so stupid. The only thing stupider than stupid is stupid with a pistol. 'Put it back in your pocket,' I told him, 'turn around.' He didn't listen. He took a shot at them. Can you imagine? Seven of them, with one shot? He'd lost his mind! He ran into the grain field then to hide. You can't hide in a grain field from men on horseback. He wasn't thinking at all. They found him, of course, and they put a rope on him and led him into the woods. We waited near the woods for him to come out. But they shot him. He...your brother...he's dead. The Russians shot your brother. I'm so sorry, Sofie."

Their mother crossed herself and gasped her distress. "And you? They didn't chase you?"

"They didn't have to. They'd made their point."

"I think we shouldn't wait any longer," Vytas confided to his father. "I think we must hide."

His father wrapped his arm around Vytas's shoulders.

"It might be you are right, Vytas. 240,000 Jews have been killed; over 500,000 Catholics have been deported, or killed. And who knows who is counting? It might be more. Time will tell. God will tell us when it is time to go. We must listen well, ja? For the moment we're fairly safe. We've been scratched from the Siberia list. Because I once did a kindness to a man in the militia, our names were scratched from that list by him. He remembered. You remember this, Vytas. God will never forget the kindnesses you do to others, no matter who they are, and you will be rewarded for it. We must thank God."

"Yes, Dad. I'll remember." *I wonder what kindness he did? But, I know, Dad would never tell even if I asked him. He'd probably say, 'Doesn't matter. God knows.'"*

Chapter 16

Warning

"How is my cousin Vincus liking college? Well enough? Does he do well living away from home? What does he say?"

Vytas looked up to answer Robert's question when he noticed movement in the field.

"Hush," he said. "Look casually behind you, Robert, but keep working."

Vytas, Jon, and their cousin Robert slowed their shoveling of the grain that morning and watched the Russian soldiers approaching.

"Look too busy to care," said Vytas quietly, and pitched another shovel of grain.

"What do they want?" whispered Jon.

"Be still," Vytas whispered back. "Let me do the talking." *Wish Vincus was here.*

The Russians approached. They held their hands in front of them, opened.

"They don't have guns," Vytas explained. "They want us to know that."

"We can't trust them," replied Jon.

"Haloo," the Russians called, halting at a distance. "We've gotten lost in the woods. Our horses are distressed. We need hay and water for the horses. Will you give us some?"

The boys looked at each other in silence.

"Wish Dad was here," murmured Jon.

"I think I know what he'd do," answered Vytas thoughtfully. "All right, then," he called to the Russians. "We can spare some hay." Then quietly to his brother and cousin he added, "Keep a safe distance from them. Don't let them near enough to grab you. Jon, slip around to the shed and get the hunting rifles. Remember that Father has begun leaving them loaded. Be careful handling them. Don't let them see you."

Jon ducked and ran through the stables. Robert waved the soldiers in.

"Thank you, then," the soldiers said, and followed the two boys into the barn. The soldiers looked around, interested in the rafters where sausages hung next to hares and foxes, and skins hung from pegs. They eyed the supply of grains. The boys put out four bales of hay and a bag of water.

"Thanks," the soldiers said again, and shouldered the supplies. Still looking around they moved slowly out of the big barn.

"They're just a bit too interested and a bit too friendly," murmured Vytas.

"I agree," Robert said.

Their Ukrainian farm hand, Petre, had watched all this unnoticed from the back of the barn. As soon as the Russians were gone he flew into the house kitchen.

"*Zhinka*," he panted. "You must warn your husband. A patrol of Russians has just come to assess your supplies. They will be back. You must leave immediately. You must warn your husband. You must all leave. I know the Russians, I know how they operate. These soldiers were not lost. They were scouting. More will be back with horses and guns. You must get word to your husband quickly."

The boys entered the kitchen in time to hear the tail end of the Ukrainian's report. They thought the boy was tattling on them for giving away the hay and they all began to explain and defend themselves.

"Quiet," demanded their mother. "Petre has warned us. We must get word to your father. Robert, take one of the horses and ride home quickly. Say nothing about this to anyone."

Robert looked puzzled, but nodded to his aunt. He glanced at his cousins and pulled his cap. "I know," he said sadly. "Good bye, then."

"I can go for Jonas," said Petre. "I know where he is today. You need to pack up." In a short while Petre and their father appeared, looking worn and worried.

86

Chapter 17

Escape

"Vytas, come here, son. You are to go into the barn, feed the horses, and hitch one horse to the wagon, but leave it in the barn. Continue to do your outside work as normal. Ignore everything you see going on around you. Act normal."

"Ja, Dad, I will do that." *What is he talking about? Work as normal ? What is going on?*

Vytas worked diligently at his chores, as he usually did, but his mind was racing. He watched to see what everyone else had been told to do. Jon was probably in the field with the hands. So far, everything seemed quite normal. Food was prepared in the kitchen; clothing was being taken care of. Everyone was absorbed in his or her work and ignored each other. Vytas fed and watered all the animals. After hitching one horse to the wagon, he went to the garden where he saw his mother and his oldest sister Jane make several trips from the kitchen to the barn carrying wrapped items. Jane stopped to hang a laundered tablecloth on the clothesline. *Working as normal?*

Vytas hoed the beet root while keeping a watchful eye on the activity. His father was still sitting at his desk with papers stacked before him. Vytas saw his mother come outside from the back door and go into the barn with an armful of blankets. She didn't return. His two younger sisters, Irena, 8, and Dona, 6, came out the front door. Irena cut flowers from the flower bed then went into the barn. Dona spoke to Jane who removed some clothes on the clothesline, folded them, then disappeared behind the barn. After while his father walked toward him.

"Give the hoe to me, Vytas. Go into the barn and give every animal another feeding and fill all the water troughs. When you have finished, go upstairs and stand in the loft so I can see you. When you see me go into the barn, come down."

"What? But, why is this?"

"We don't have time for questions now. Do as I tell you. You must trust me. We don't know who may be watching." Vytas handed his father the hoe and went into the barn. All was very quiet. He knew his mother and his three sisters were already in the barn, he had seen them enter. *Where can they be?* He fed the animals again and filled the troughs with water. It was too quiet. He discovered Irena's flowers tucked into the bridle of the hitched horse. *I see; a horse going merrily down the road on family business, looking normal. We don't know who is watching. I understand. With the girls coming and going, it would be hard to keep track of everyone.*

"Vytas," his name was whispered. He jumped in surprise to see Jon crawl out from under the wagon. Jon hopped onto the tail of the wagon and dove into the straw.

"Cover me with the gunny bags," he whispered. Vytas lifted the bags and discovered they were filled with folded blankets. He did as he was told, but unanswered questions swirled in his head like a storm over the Baltic Sea. It was then he noticed Jane's red boot sticking out of the potato sacks and blankets. He picked it up and discovered it was attached to her foot.

"What is—

"Shush. Cover me," she whispered. "We're hiding. It's sort of a game. We're hiding from Dad, aren't we girls." He heard giggles of the little girls from under the straw and potato sacks. Vytas quickly piled the heavy potato sacks over her foot. *So this is where everyone is? In the wagon? A game? So that's what she's told the little girls. That's why they aren't afraid.*

He ran up to the loft and looked down at his father hoeing. They nodded slightly to each other. He closed the shutters and returned. His father came into the barn.

"Well, then, off for the market, eh, Vytas?" he said louder than necessary. Vytas noticed Vincas' hunting rifle hidden under the wagon seat. He was sure the others were somewhere near within quick reach.

"Dad, what about Grandfather?" Vytas asked quietly.

"Your grandfather wishes to remain with the farm. We must honor his decision. He will be safe. Most likely. Take this. Handle it carefully."

Vytas stared at the Lueger, bit his lip, and put the gun in his pocket. *This is no game.*

The wagon pulled out of the barn less than three hours after Petre the Ukrainian had warned them. Vytas watched the farm getting smaller as the horse trotted down the road away from the barn, the granary, the fields…away from everything he knew and loved.

June was always an exciting time of year for farmers as the fields and trees were new again and the garden was producing. Birds were singing and the river ran cold and fresh. *Could we postpone this game?* No. In his heart he knew…this was not a game.

They traveled one and a half miles to another village and spent the night with their father's cousin. In the morning their trek would begin for real. Vytas was fourteen years old and this was the beginning of a great adventure into the unknown. They were headed for the German border. He thought he wasn't afraid –yet.

Chapter 18

On The Road

As they moved on the next day, different refugees attached themselves to Vytas' family. Soon there were quite a few family wagons and walkers moving together. The children no longer needed to hide now they were away from their village. Friends and neighbors could tell the truth: they hadn't seen the family leave. No one knew where they'd gone.

All the families were armed with hunting guns in their wagons, and handguns in their pockets. There was safety in numbers, they hoped.

Late in the afternoon after walking all day, they saw a woman standing by the edge of the road.

"Please help me," she begged. "My husband is a forester. He's hiding because two Russians came to our place demanding food. I have none. They would have killed me except they saw your wagons coming with all of you. They ran off into the forest. Please take us with you."

The woman climbed into Jonas's wagon and directed them to where her husband was hiding. The forester offered his bicycle to Vytas, who accepted it readily and pedaled alongside the wagon.

"We are going to Dotnuva," Jonas told them. "My son Vincus is in college there and he is waiting for us."

They drove through Dotnuva to the outskirts of town where they set up a primitive camp in the fields. Vytas hopped on his bike and pedaled back to town. Vincas was to meet him at the government building in the center of the town square as planned.

He stopped in front of the steps of the large formal building. Vincas wasn't there. Vytas sat on the step with his bike leaning against the steps next to him. He sprawled in the sunshine to wait.

"I need your bike. Let me borrow it."

Vytas opened his eyes and blinked into the sun. A German police officer stood close to Vytas's bike.

"I can't give it to you. It isn't mine."

"I need it," the policeman snarled.

"I need it, too, and it isn't mine."

The policeman had his fat hands wrapped around the handlebars. Vytas studied the man's jaw and saw confrontation. If he went for his gun, he'd have to let go of the bike.

The policeman yanked the bike; Vytas yanked back. The policeman tried to wrestle the bike free from Vytas, who clung stubbornly to the handlebars.

"You can't have it," Vytas growled through his teeth.

"What's going on?" asked Vincas. "You there, policeman. You've nothing better to do than to bully a poor farm boy for his bike? Shame on you, man. A fine look for a German police officer."

The red-faced policeman let up on the bike; Vytas didn't. He jerked the bicycle free from the policeman and lifted it to his other side. With one hand on his pocket, and now standing tall, he dared the policeman to come after it. The policeman glared up at Vincas who towered over him. He assessed his position: two tall, strong young men, possibly armed, against him alone. He backed off, turned, and walked quickly away. The brothers smiled their relief.

"Just in time," said Vytas. "Thanks."

They camped in the dark forests at night and walked in the daylight, for the next five days, stopping only to feed and water the horse. The forests were crawling with Russian bandits. Everyone held tight to their weapons.

When they reached a place to camp with a friendly farmer they stayed there for two weeks. They hunted for their food and they helped the farmer with his work.

Then one day Vytas said, "Dad, I hear something." They all listened to the distant rumbling getting closer, louder. Jon looked to the clear blue sky.

"I don't think it's thunder, Dad."

"I don't think it is either, boys." Jonas moved swiftly to locate the farmer. "Gather the others," he told his sons.

"What is it, Jonas?" his wife asked.

"They are coming. We must leave now to stay ahead of the fighting. The German tanks are coming." They quickly broke camp, packed their wagons and moved on. The farmer and his daughter joined the traveling refugees. They tossed their few treasures into a small handcart, and walked away from their home. The farmer's daughter's brave tears left telltale smudges on her cheeks, but she held her head high, plodding along next to her father, beside Vytas's family.

Later that day, in July, 1944, they came to the river, the border into East Prussia (Germany). Hundreds of refugees, wagons, and retreating German soldiers clotted the wide road, which narrowed suddenly to cross the footbridge.

"Looks like a big log jam, Dad," Vytas said.

"Patience. We're all going the same place, and all in a hurry."

It took all day for the mass of people to cross the narrow bridge.

Once across the bridge, the narrow road again spread out into the wide main thoroughfare. The column of people looked miles long and a mile wide to Vytas. *So many people, as far as I can see, a sea of people.*

"Pull to the side of the road," his Dad said to the others in their group. "This road looks too dangerous to me. I think we should give up the main road and travel on the minor roads or go cross country through the woods. We need to get away from here. This column is a sitting duck."

"What about bandits roaming in the woods?" Some of the travelers in their group questioned Jonas' opinion and argued with him.

"Don't you think it would be safer to keep traveling with the crowd?"

"I don't think so," Jonas said. "Something is telling me. Come or not, but I'm taking my family a different way."

"It will take longer, we should stay on the main highway. It's quicker that way."

"It won't be safe to be a small group, off by yourself. There's bandits, you know. You should stay with the crowd, Jonas. Ja, we'll be better to stay with the crowd."

"We are going now," was Jonas's final answer. He turned his family's wagon and crossed into a field to find a secondary road. A few of the group followed him, the rest returned to the crowded main road.

Jonas found a bumpy, dusty, secondary road. It would be slower and more uncomfortable for sure. But Jonas felt this was safer. They'd traveled only about a mile and half when they heard loud thundering, roaring, rumbling, followed by screaming, and staccato blasts of machine gun fire and exploding earth. Behind them to the west they saw the Russian bombers strafing the main road, killing the retreating German soldiers, and the innocent refugees.

"Sitting ducks," gasped Vytas. "Father was right. How did he know?"

The little wagon train pulled off the road into the trees and tall grasses and stood still as statuary. When the planes had gone, all that was left was screaming and moaning in clouds of smoke. Some in Jonas's group vomited. Others dropped to their knees in prayer. Some sobbed. Others keened. Vytas sat stunned in silence. *Murder. It was murder.* His mother crossed herself as tears dripped off her chin. A murmur, a soft litany of unified prayer hummed through the otherwise silent forest. Vytas listened. Silence. *Not a sound. Even the birds are at prayer. Like requiem.*

Chapter 19

Soviet Occupation

After another day of hiking along the isolated road, they met a gestapo, a German policeman, who spoke Lithuanian. He traveled with them and led them to a barn in a village. He told them the wives and children would be allowed to stay in the farmhouse, the men could stay in the barn. The next day he led them to a "distribution point" where they would be given work assignments by the German government. Vytas imagined the distribution point would be a government building. The distribution point turned out to be a field. They were given their work assignments. Jonas and his family were to go to a farm as part of the work force.

"This is a good assignment for our family," Vytas heard his father tell the gestapo. "We are used to farm work. We are hard-working, successful farmers. The work isn't our complaint."

"What is our complaint, then, Dad?" Vytas asked, after the gestapo had gone.

"That we are working as slaves for the Germans who are supposed to be our friends who say they are protecting us."

The summer passed pleasantly with the farm work being familiar to their family. They had food, shelter, safety, and worthwhile work. They were alive. They were grateful.

When November came they heard the distant guns again. Jonas went into the town and applied for travel permission, which was granted.

"It's time for us to move," he told his family. The family gathered their things. The German farmer was angry to hear this.

"Your work assignment is not over. You cannot leave. I won't permit it."

"We have travel permission. Here is our government documentation. We are free to leave."

The farmer sputtered unhappily, while Vincas packed their wagon.

"You cannot have the horse and wagon, then," the farmer said.

"It's my father's horse and wagon," Vincas reminded him.

"You are breaking your work assignment contract. I'm keeping the horse and wagon as compensation." Vincas went to find his father.

"We are traveling by rail to Dresden," Jonas explained. "We only need the wagon and horse to get to the rail station. You can come with us and bring the horse and wagon back."

"No," he answered firmly. "The horse and wagon are mine now, and they aren't for loan. Hurry up and leave."

No amount of reason changed his mind. The farmer who had been so kind to them for four months shocked the family with this spiteful behavior. They unloaded the wagon, repacked, and prepared to walk the mile and a half to the rail station, carrying everything they owned.

On the train, Vytas watched his dad sitting quietly with a vacant expression, and wondered if he was afraid or nervous, or maybe just tired. *I think he's wondering what is the future for this family? Is there a future?*

His mother looked out the window and said nothing. Vincas and Jon chewed their nails and mumbled to each other. The girls sat with their eyes closed. A thought niggled at Vytas: *something is going to happen.* Out the window he could see the shadow of the skyline of Berlin approaching in the distance.

The evening sky looked peaceful enough; the train began speeding up. Everyone relaxed. They'd soon be in Berlin.

Chapter 20

The Sky is Falling

The brakes screamed. The sky lit up as in a summer storm, blotting out the stars. Over the screech of the locomotive wheels, tremendous explosions with booms and crashes erupted in the night sky searing brilliant holes in the darkness. Air raid sirens wailed. Red arrows zipped across the sky. The train skidded to a halt while the air around them exploded in staccato bursts. The train cars rocked to and fro, the engine started and stopped. The train lurched forward, then backward, the engineer unsure which way to go. Jane and Irena tried to look out the window but Jonas pulled them away from the window and pushed them and his wife into the center aisle where other travelers dropped quickly and quietly away from the windows. There was no panic; the passengers were numb with fear. *This is the end for us*, Vytas, thought. *The end of my family. God have mercy on us all.*

The train began moving in the opposite direction. *It's going too fast too soon*, Vytas thought. The explosions continued and the train seemed to be trying to outrun them. Then with another sudden screech, the brakes jerked and the wheels skidded along the rails again. Passengers sat stunned and quiet. When the train halted suddenly, the people fell on top of each other in a lurch of momentum.

The bombs continued to fall over Berlin all night while, in the dark, the passengers prayed, knowing the German rail lines were being targeted by the British bombers. When the bombing ceased, everything out the windows was very dark except for the glow of many fires all around them. Vytas's mother clutched her amber rosary beads in her fist. The girls joined her, murmuring their familiar prayers for comfort. All through the train, whispered Lithuanian prayer sustained the refugees.

As dawn awakened the desolate, smoking scene around Berlin, the passengers were still not allowed off the train. They could see workers on the rails trying to repair enough line to move the train. Armed soldiers lined the tracks on both sides of the train.

"Dad, how will we get out of Berlin?"

His father looked at him, then looked away at the scene. There was no doubt about it. His father was afraid. Vytas was afraid, too.

As the pale and shaken passengers began moving about, a long queue grew at the toilet doors.

Women began unwrapping bits of food they'd saved for their families. Trembling voices reassured one another they were still alive.

When the train finally jerked its way into Dresden they were informed the distribution point was at a camp one mile away. Gathering their belongings, the passengers all walked to the camp, led by a gestapo. They kept a watchful eye on the sky and all around them. They moved into a barracks full of bugs and people, hidden behind a barbed wire fence.

"Dad, are we the enemy?" asked Irena.

"We're no one's enemy," he answered. "Things have just gotten confusing that's all. It will be okay." Vytas felt a shiver of uncertainty in his spine.

"It looks like we're prisoners," Jane whispered quietly.

Two weeks went by before they were given their work assignments in Sebnitz. Vytas was too young to work and was disappointed he wouldn't be leaving every day with his dad, two brothers and sister Jane when they left for the parachute factory. The factory was a silk mill where the silk for the German parachutes was woven.

Eventually they were given a nice apartment across the street from the factory. Their food staples were rationed, salads were already prepared. Coal briquettes were for cooking, and oil squeezed from the coal was used to make gasoline. Every night Blackout was strictly enforced. They drew black curtains across all windows and doors, lights were extinguished. Glow-in-the-dark buttons were issued and worn pinned on their shirts so they didn't run into each other in the dark. The city was black and still, waiting for the morning.

Danute 1944

Chapter 21

October

Danute spent more and more time alone in her room as autumn blew into their town. She hated all the talk about the Russians and the disappearing people. She buried her head in her pillow when street riots broke out below her window. Her mother stayed close to home and everyone was tense. The life she had always known had disappeared along with many of their friends and relatives.

Her father suggested the children should go through the woods to their uncle's farm. It was on the outskirts of town and would be a safer place to be if the Russians "cleansed" their town of Catholics. The children put on a few layers of clothing so they wouldn't have to carry anything, and early in the chilly morning took off on foot for their uncle's home. The thick woods of Simkaiciai would be their cover.

Ahead of them in a break in the woods, the sun beamed through, casting moving shadows.

"Stop," Danute whispered. "I see something."

"Ja, I too," said Victor. "Can you feel something?"

"The ground is shaking," said Ilona. "Listen. What is that noise?"

Rumbling like a big hungry belly, the ground trembled beneath them.

"Like an earthquake," whispered Victor.

As if the forest suddenly became alive, Russian soldiers bolted from the trees and hurled themselves to the ground. German tanks came barreling through the forest snapping saplings and churning up the earth. The Russians began shooting and yelling. The children screamed and ran for home. Out of breath and trembling in fear, the children tried to tell their tale.

"It's the Germans. They are here!" panted Victor breathlessly.

"We will be free now; they will make the Russians leave, won't they?" Ilona looked hopefully at her parents.

"The tanks are coming right now. They are coming through the woods into town," Danute explained excitedly. The family didn't know whether to laugh or cry, rejoice or flee. All this time they had waited for the German army to come to their aid. Now they were here. This was good news; wasn't it?

The powerful Russian front moved quickly across Lithuania. Terrifying rumors became reality. A patriotic man while fleeing his home saw a picture of Stalin in a window. He grabbed the picture, but before he could rip it apart, he was shot. Old stories from old soldiers in World War I were told as warnings to the younger families. They'd seen it all before.

Danute's grandfather, who lived with her aunt and uncle, had been a border guard in World War I. He told his war stories, too. He warned them never to get caught stealing.

"Russians have no tolerance for theft," he said. "I saw a ten year-old starving girl, trying to catch a goose, be shot as an example to thieves. It will be repeated here, now" he warned.

Danute shuddered and vowed not to steal anyone's goose, even if she were starving.

Lithuanians left everything they had and fled to stay ahead of the advancing armies. They abandoned their homes to find food and shelter in unlikely places. The German army was trying to rout Russia from captive Lithuania. But, they were putting all able bodied Lithuanian men in German work camps. The Lithuanians were captive, ungrateful slaves of their liberators. The Russians continued to kill and deport the Lithuanians.

Danute's father Petras was walking on the road near their house in the late afternoon with Kent, when German soldiers came from behind a building and surprised them. Their guns were aimed at Petras.

"Move," they said. "You are invited to a party. We're taking you."

Anele came flying out the door screaming. "Go away. He can't go with you." Kent was frightened by her hysterical voice.

"It's okay, Mother. Calm down. Look, Gestapo, I will go with you. Leave my father here to care for my mother. She's not well. I'll go in his place."

"Oh, ja? Well, well. You're a good sport, heh? A hero, ja? The more the merrier. We'll make a good party, ja?" The Germans laughed and pushed both the men with their guns.

"Hands up!" They marched the two men down the street. Neighbors watched, crossing themselves behind the curtains, knowing they could be next.

Petras and Kent were held in a work camp outside the town digging trenches for the Germans, while the family, afraid and suspicious, stayed at their uncle's old farmhouse. Other families were split up also, but Danute's independent mother Anele wouldn't hear of it.

"We are family. We live as one family. We may die as one family, but we will not be split up. I will have a plan to reunite us."

The children maintained a prayer novena for their father and brother Kent, while their mother Anele devised her plan. Somehow, during the night, Anele got hold of some rare bacon.

"Mother? Please...be careful," pleaded Danute. "We shall pray for you."

Anele left her children at the farm house and walked several miles to the work camp. It was a desolate walk through bomb craters. Barbed wire and other detritus of war surrounded her. She ignored the stench of smoke, ruin, and death, and stumbled along in the tracks dug deep by the German tanks. The air was dank and putrid. Anele barely noticed. She thought only of reuniting her family. She entered the work camp unharmed. Her husband and son were delighted to see her, but they feared for her.

"Mother, you should not have come. Traveling isn't safe."

"How will you get home?" her husband asked.

"The Germans are our friends, are they not? Why shouldn't I be safe here?" she questioned. "You'll see," she said. "Who is the camp leader?" Kent pointed out the commander of the camp. Anele approached him and covertly removed the bacon from her purse and showed it to him. Kent and Petras watched as she pointed them out to the commander. With their heads down and their voices muted, the commander and Anele struck a deal.

"Come, Petras," she said to her husband. "Come along, Kent. The commander will allow you to walk partway down the road with me."

"What? Why would they do that?"

"Father, no, we shouldn't. It's a trick. I've seen them shoot men in the back if they even thought they were walking away. The commander may be setting us up."

Anele turned, smiled, and waved prettily at the commander, who returned the wave and smiled.

"There, you see? Now, come on, hurry up."

They walked a distance before Petras said, "This is probably far enough, Anele."

"Just a bit farther," Anele begged. They walked several yards more.

"A little more," she said.

"Mother, how much bacon did you bribe him with?"

"Enough," she answered, and urged them on. Across the barren land laid waste by the implements of war, the men continued to fear. Anele, driven by the need to reunite her family didn't have room for fear.

They reached the farmhouse exhausted from their vigorous walk. Danute, Victor, and Ilona were beside themselves with joy and relief. They had prepared a camouflaged hideout for the men. Inside one of the large barns filled with hay, they prepared a tunnel through the haystacks carefully hidden from sight. They hid the men in the tunnel. People were watching, they knew. It was going to be difficult to deliver any food to the barn. It would have to be delivered disguised as something else. Finders reported their neighbors and were rewarded by the Germans with extra food rations or favors. No one could be trusted. The children spoke to no one and Anele joined them as they continued their novena. Days passed and the Germans did not come to retake their father and Kent.

"Enough time has passed," their father said. "If the Germans were coming to get us, they would have been here by now. Enough time has passed to avoid suspicion. Tonight we leave. No one will have to lie for us. No one will know when or where our family went; no one saw us go."

It was a cold and rainy October night when they loaded a small wagon and headed toward Prussia. In the back of the wagon Danute's brothers hid in the mattresses. Anyone over the age of fourteen would be grabbed for the work force in Germany. Found hiding, they would be shot. The tall, skinny fourteen year-old girl, feared for her brothers' lives, and shivered in the rain.

Chapter 22

Stranded

The Russian army was advancing. The whole world seemed to be under bombardment. Shells exploded everywhere and refugees clogged the roads out of the country. The sounds of creaking wagon wheels and clomping hooves were their constant companions. Bent, weary, anguished, and fearful, the Lithuanians moved west away from the Russian front with scarce food and bare existence. Bikes, trains, cars, wagons, miniature farm wagons pulled by humans, all ages, walking; everyone was moving away from the front lines toward Germany.

The Germans were retreating on the same roads and took up more than half the road, leaving only part of one side for the refugees. If the refugees got in their way, they beat or shot them. The refugees watched in horror, realizing that their liberator had turned out to be yet another brutal captor, no more friend than Russia.

"Who is our enemy?" everyone was asking.

When the column reached the border of East Prussia, Petras hesitated.

"I can't do it. I won't. I can't be pushed out of my homeland. I'm not leaving. I've got to go back."

"No!" his wife commanded. Her hands flew to cover her ears.

Bombs exploded. The refugees dropped into the dirt and covered their heads. Debris rained down on them, while stones and dirt flew skyward. The air they breathed became clogged and thick with smoke. Flames licked the ground. The bridge they'd crossed only a moment ago vanished. It was demolished by the Germans to prevent the refugees from going back into their country, just as Petras had decided to do a moment ago. Petras dropped his head.

"We have no country," he whispered. Tears raced down his cheeks. "God help us. Hell has been opened." Around them people moaned and shrubbery burned. Scorched, splintered bridge pieces crashed into the river.

"They'll not kill this family," Anele asserted. "Get up." Danute popped right up, brushed herself off. She wanted to be as certain of everything as her mother. She shook the crud from her braids, smearing ash across her face. She looked skyward. "God help us."

The refugees in Prussia were kept in the town until the Germans put them on a train with other refugees. The train went to Gdansk, Poland. There, about two hundred of them spent two nights in a school, while the Germans decided where to send them next. The German Salvation Army came to the train station with weak bouillon to feed the masses of people.

"There are too many people here," the Salvation Army workers said. "No place can house and feed so many people."

"That's not our fault," grumbled Anele.

"They can't stay in Poland," the Salvation Army worker told the soldiers. "Take them away."

"Mother, what are they going to do with us?" Danute whispered.

"I don't think we want to know, daughter."

"There is no room on the train. Only Germans, wounded, and soldiers. Everyone else, walk," the commandant said.

The column moved for weeks, walking and walking. No one knew where they were headed. They slept in abandoned barns and ate whatever they could find or beg. When they at last made it to a large town that had a train station, they were told they could take a refugee train into Germany.

The crush of people charged the train, pushing and shoving, everyone hoping to find room on the train. The crowded people slept on rope baggage racks, and outside in the cold on the coupling platforms. It was so crowded they rode standing up. People falling asleep on their feet, were held upright by the wall of others surrounding them. They crisscrossed Germany many times, barely getting off the train. No one wanted them. There wasn't room anywhere for this massive influx of refugees. They stayed on the train.

The train moved at night with no lights, and they stopped for the day hiding the train in tunnels where the refugees stood in long lines for the Salvation Army's watery soup. They left Poland, passed through Germany to the border of Holland, then back again while rail lines continued to be destroyed, repaired, and destroyed again. Refugees flooded towns and countries. The soldiers stood at all the stations. The refugees could not debark. There was no room for them anywhere. When they finally were allowed off the train, they didn't know where they were, or how long they would be there. The Salvation Army led the huge ragged crowd of refugees to an abandoned warehouse where they dispensed more watery soup.

Stranded now, inside Germany, the children squinted into the sky at American and British bombers battling the Luftwafte over Germany. Sometimes the planes roared directly overhead. Occasionally someone pointed out parachutes popping open in the distance, silhouetted against the sour sky. The horizon in every direction glowed orange. Columns of black smoke like funeral pyres billowed skyward. The refugees were numb, hungry, and homesick. But, they weren't sure exactly where home was anymore. They also weren't sure who their allies or enemies were.

Eventually another train came for them. Some workers were hauled to Stuttgart, Germany. Danute and her family rolled on to Vezel, Germany, where more bombs awaited them. The train lumbered on.

Chapter 23

Christmas Everywhere

In Ausig, Czechoslavakia, Danute's family was one of five Lithuanian families placed in a large empty building they thought might have once been part of a brewery. It had cement floors, one window, and a triple bunk that held six people. The room was crowded with 400 women and children. The men were separated from their families and held in another building. There was one stove for all the families to cook on. Children were hungry late into the night waiting for their mothers' turn at the stove.

The bugs in the room were terrifying to city-girl Danute who had never seen so many kinds of bugs, and hated every one. Her smooth, pale complexion was red and rough. Welts were scabby. Her body and her head itched and burned with tiny bugs. She scratched her skin raw.

The refugees weren't treated badly, just as an inconvenience. In stores the Germans served their own people first, which meant not much was left for the refugees. Even though they were issued food cards from the Red Cross, there wasn't food available. The Salvation Army continued to bring the watery broth. Skinny Danute was getting skinnier.

"This is our first Christmas away from home," her mother complained. "God willing, it is our last. Ever! We *will* be home again."

Danute began salvaging the paper labels from canned goods and kept them pressed under her mattress.

"What are you collecting the trash for?" her mother asked.

Danute just smiled and shrugged. It was her secret.

"It's Christmas, Mama."

"Ja, so, in this ugly place, Christmas won't be Christmas."

"I think Christmas can be anywhere. And in this ugly place it's more important, more welcome. Don't you think so, Mama?"

"Such a silly girl."

"I'm not silly. I imagine Jesus was born in an ugly place like this. I'll bet it even had bugs."

"That's blasphemous, Danute."

The women and children practiced traditional Lithuanian carols to sing on Christmas Day, and Danute sang joyfully, trying to forget the bleakness surrounding her.

Using whatever food they could find, the women served their meals on Christmas Day calling the food by traditional Lithuanian holiday names, vinegretas, meats, herring, tortes, all their favorite recipes, pretending it was something wonderful, and presenting it on tin and cardboard as a feast fitting the King.

"If you call it this, it will taste like it," the mothers explained to their hungry children.

"Tastes like water to me," complained a child.

"Water is good for you," all the mothers answered together.

"Now it's time for Christmas surprises," announced Danute. She passed out her Christmas greeting cards drawn and written on the backs of the canned foods labels. Some of the edges were cut in scallops, some in fringe. Some were folded into colorful shapes. But all had a greeting and a little picture that Danute had drawn. The displaced people stared at her. Eventually, some of the women smiled, and patted her. Some wiped away a tear before it escaped.

"Thanks, Danute. Nice."

"Ja. It's good Christmas."

"Christmas is always good, ja? Thank you, Danute for reminding us of that."

After Christmas more Lithuanians arrived from Breslau, Poland, making the room even more crowded. Some of the newcomers had news of others who had vanished, escaped, or emigrated. Mostly the news was greeted with moans and tears. Rarely was the news good news. Danute and her family lived in Ausig for six months.

Chapter 24

Betrayed

A Lutheran minister eventually came into their camp.

"The Russian front is near and there's no place to go. Take the clothes you have and go to the train station and see what happens. You cannot stay here," he warned the refugees. "You must get out now."

"They say there is no room on the train again," Petras said to his family. "But, quickly, get your things and come. I have an idea." The family pushed their way through the madding crowd onto the train platform, where the conductor struggled to maintain control.

"No room!" he shouted. "Go away!" He swung his arms and pushed people off the platform, shoving them onto the tracks and into each other. A porter helped him by sweeping people off the platform with a broom.

Danute's father went to the front of the train carrying a bundle under his arm wrapped in a towel. He waived to the engineer and motioned for him to come and see what he had. Curious, the engineer climbed down.

"You, there. What do you want? What have you got there?"

Petras unwrapped his treasure and showed it to the engineer.

"A fine radio," he said.

"Ja, I see it's a very fine radio. Very nice indeed." The engineer agreed that in exchange for the radio, he could find a place for Petras's family. Petras signaled his family to approach the engine. Trying not to be noticed by the crowd, they moved casually one at a time. The engineer told them they were going to Germany. He buried them in the pile of coal in the train's engine. When all were buried, he took the radio, and started the train engine. Hordes of people screamed and pushed, trying to get on the moving, over-crowded train in panic-fed terror.

"Get away," screamed the conductor, waving his arms. "You will get run over. Stay back!" He pushed them away with his hands and feet. Still the refugees fought each other to get close to the moving train.

Under the pile of coal, Danute's eyes watered and streamed. Coal dust entered her nose and burned her throat as she breathed. She heard her family members in the darkness clear the coal dust out of their throats, trying not to cough. Her mother was a chain smoker with a chronic cough and bad lungs. Danute wondered how her mother could breathe at all under the coal. Victor sneezed. Ilona sniffled. Danute felt a sudden shift in the coal pile as the train picked up speed. The coal weighed heavy on her thin body. She ached. She tried to keep her eye lids shut tight to keep the coal dust from getting into her eyes. She could see nothing, heard only the rumbling of the engine, and felt the vibrations of the wheels. With her eyes closed, and breathing in short shallow breaths, she fought motion sickness, swallowing down the gathering saliva, coated in coal dust.

After a rather short ride, the train stopped abruptly. Danute heard angry German voices shouting. The coal pile started to shift. The family coughed as they were dragged one by one out of the pile of coal by German soldiers. The conductor stood smiling, holding his radio under his arm, and a reward from the Germans in his other hand. The family was thrown off the train with nothing, including their radio. They were surrounded by other refugees from other countries who scorned the filthy Lithuanian family, covered in coal dust, who had caused them even more inconvenience.

For many more nights they rode trains without knowing where they were or where they were going. Whenever the train stopped they were told, "This is a German resettlement camp." German refugees all got off the train.

"But, you aren't Germans. You can't stay here," they told the Lithuanians. The Lithuanians stayed on and rode the train again.

All through the long night the bombs fell. The snow on the ground was black. Singed paper and debris blew through the air like black snowflakes. The asphalt fried, the air smelled terrible of sulfur, soot, and smoke. Trees splintered, people melted into the pavement, buildings disintegrated, iron structures gone molten. The people who could move didn't know where to go, or where they were. Such was the sight that greeted Danute and her family when day dawned over Dresden, Germany. There was nothing to say. They covered their noses and mouths with their dirty hands. Confusion. So much confusion, her brain couldn't sort it out.

After several more nights on the train, the refugees were taken back to a collection point in the Russian zone.

"They are out of ideas," her mother said. "They don't know what to do with us."

"They say they are going to return all of us to our original countries," said Kent.

"Shall we believe that?" sighed Petras.

"Our home isn't safe. If we go back, what was all this for? Only to return to be killed?" Kent said angrily. "No, Father, we cannot go home. Don't even think of it."

"Maybe there's nothing left there," his mother said. Danute shuddered. She tried to remember how her house in the city looked. She remembered only her book in the wardrobe. Other memories were distant and slowly vanishing. Her memory of many cities now blurred together with her memory of Kaunas. She thought briefly of Sofyia, Bopka, and Nora. Then her thoughts returned to the moment and survival.

Chapter 25

American Zone

At the collection point into the American occupied area, most of the refugees were Polish with very few Lithuanians. An American Lieutenant stood up, and speaking Lithuanian, asked if there were any Lithuanians. Kent jumped up quickly, hand waving in the air.

"Come here. I'll be back tomorrow," the Lieutenant told him privately. "I will do everything possible to get you out."

The next day Lieutenant Adams returned with canned food. He made traveling documents for all the Lithuanians.

"In one week, on a Sunday, I'll be guarding here, and I'll take you out of camp. Leave your things hidden next to the fence. When I come, you must do as I say." He spoke quietly in Lithuanian.

With their nervousness and excitement it was hard to keep their secret or not seem too happy. Danute tried to avoid making eye contact with her brothers because one of them would burst out in happy laughter. *I can't believe it, we will finally be free. Well, at least I hope that's what we'll be. Maybe we'll just be dead.*

Sunday finally arrived. Their few belongings stashed by the fence looked like all the other trash and garbage blown and forgotten, snagged by the barbed wire. No one was the wiser when an army cleaning detail picked it up and drove it away.

The American Lieutenant Adams returned. Acting angry and bullish he yanked the Lithuanians out, as if it were a random selection and shoved them to the fence. He marched them at gun point, hands up out through the fence and into a waiting truck. The Lithuanians feigned fear and surprise. The Poles watched through the barbed wire fence, fearing for the Lithuanian refugees, but glad it wasn't them.

"Certain death," they murmured.

When the truck had left the camp, the refugees cried with relief and kissed the American lieutenant.

"You are on your way to the American Zone. There will be plenty of food and clothing for you there."

With deep sighs of resignation, they wondered if they dared hope for all that.

"Cheers to Amer-i-ca," shouted one of the men, shaking his clasped hands above his head.

"Ja, cheers," everyone agreed.

The truck driver held up his hand and made a V sign with his fingers. It was a familiar gesture to the American soldiers who'd seen Winston Churchill make it a number of times. But the Lithuanians, who'd been captives for most of the war, hadn't seen it before.

Victory? For who? Danute wondered. *Did someone win?*

The convoy of American army trucks drove them to Nuremberg, where that night they slept in a bombed out trolley car. For the next month Danute's family lived in the empty home of a French family who had fled Nuremburg.

Her father corresponded with his old army buddies who warned him, "Never leave the American Zone. It is the only safe quarter. No matter how bad it seems, it's better than anywhere else. The Germans are not our allies. The Russians are not our protectorates. And the Nazis are the enemy of the world."

Danute and Vytas 1945

Chapter 26

Danute in Camp

Outside the American Zone on a gray and dismal April day, goose-stepping Nazi armies paraded in the streets of Germany in mourning of Adolf Hitler's death. Secret smiles, fingers crossed, and feelings of hope buoyed the spirits of the refugees, safe inside the American Zone. Would their homes soon be safe? Without Hitler will the Nazis quit? It was their unspoken prayer.

"Will the war be over now?" Ilona wanted to know.

"I'm not sure how we'd know exactly," answered Danute.

"Everything sort of looks the same every day. But the Nazis have lost their leader. That can only be good news for us," Victor said.

"Nothing seems to be different, not really," Danute complained.

"It took a long time for Europe to get in this shape; I suppose it will take a while to get it back," her father answered. "A bit more patience."

"Patience. Patience he says. How can we find any more patience?" Anele complained. Danute knew her mother's poor health was depleting her energy.

After one month, the American soldiers put Danute's family on a train headed for a United Nations displaced persons' camp in Hanau near Frankfort, Germany. It was formerly a German army facility. There, they were told, they would have food, shelter, and medicine.

The camp was like a small city. Large brick army barracks, some three stories tall, lined the center street. Buildings that had been factories, still full of boxes of nuts, bolts, and machine parts, were partially bombed out and now sat abandoned.

The camp was set up with schools, doctors' offices, a post office, and a store. A total of 3500 resident refugees lived in the buildings.

The Baltic displaced persons--Latvians, Estonians, and Lithuanians,--were kept separate from the Slavic Poles, Czechs, and Yugoslavs, though none of them knew why.

"Do you think the Americans think we don't like each other?" Danute asked.

"Who knows what they think," Anele answered.

"At this point, what is their reason for keeping us apart? We are all the same--homeless, poor, sick, hungry. Why do we care?" another woman answered.

"Hah! I think we all have better things to think about than disliking our neighbors. But, who knows what the Americans think of us." Anele shrugged and half smiled at her daughter. "They live on the other side of the world. What do they know of us?"

A staffed kitchen, once equipped to serve an army, now served rice soup and other meager meals to the displaced people, who helped with their own meal preparation.

"I think I'm the fastest and best potato peeler in the camp," Danute announced. "We should have a contest."

"Don't let it go to your head," her mother said.

"It's all right for her to have pride," said another woman. "It's all right, child. You can be proud of anything you do well, peeling potatoes, or emptying the slops, running in Olympics, or singing a song. Do it well, and be a proud Lithuanian."

"Such talk," her mother grumped.

"Well, anyway, I'm hungry, so I'm peeling fast. I'm really hungry."

"Offer your hunger up in prayer," the woman said. "Like the saints and the martyrs do."

"Will that make my hunger go away?"

"No, but it will give your hunger a purpose, so you'll feel better about being hungry. You can forget feeling bad."

"Oh. Is that what you do, too, Mama?"

"No. I'm not a saint and I've no patience with martyrs. Stop talking so much and get those potatoes ready. Pay attention to your job or you will waste too much potato. Thin. Very thin skin, Danute. Scrape, don't peel."

"Let the child have a moment of joy, Anele. God knows we could all do with some happy chatter."

"I can raise my own daughter, thank you."

Danute paused and studied the exchange between her mother and the other woman. *This woman has known a harder life than Mama. Maybe this is easier for her. Mama isn't used to being tied to the kitchen. She's used to coming and going as she wishes. This is harder for her. Perhaps I'll be like both of them. I think when people live so close together they get grumpy. Mama isn't used to being close to people.*

Several families shared the large rooms, and privacy was a matter of hanging army blankets over clothesline ropes between their areas.

Danute's family moved three times within this camp. The first room they had was converted to a doctor's office. The second room they shared with a spiteful German woman who blamed them for her hardship.

"My country would have food enough for all Germans if it wasn't for those outsiders like you taking it all," she grumbled. The third was a smaller room with bunked beds, but at least they were alone.

"Good," Danute said. "If I have to listen to snoring, it will be my own family snoring in Lithuanian."

Danute contributed by doing many of the household chores. Her mother, 49, continuously ill from congestive heart failure and lifelong smoking, seemed to gather strength whenever the family needed her, but she was weak and ill otherwise.

Her father was 59. He belonged to many different Catholic charitable organizations and worked long hours in a basement organizing donations and CARE packages for distribution among the European refugees. He prayed with thanksgiving for his family's safety. Danute noticed how thin he'd gotten, and how hard he worked.

"We couldn't have survived without the American intervention," their father told them often. "Don't ever forget that."

Vytas

Chapter 27

Displaced Persons

At the time Danute's family was being transported to Nuremburg, Vytas's family was on the train to Bamberg to find work on farms in nearby Trabelsdorf.

Vincus spoke passable German so he went into the village to find work for all of them. Their mother, father, and two sisters found a small home to live in. Vytas and Vincus each found a place to live and work. Vytas lived upstairs in a carpenter's house, and was to help the carpenter who made coffins. He held lumber while it was cut and swept sawdust, but he was unclear what else he was to do. So with time on his hands, he made a pair of dice out of scrap wood. Though they were well crafted, the carpenter was unimpressed and passed Vytas off to a farmer. He worked on the farm and lived upstairs in the farmer's house.

A couple months later in April the American army fired two warning shots into the village. No one was injured although the roof was blown off the building where Jon was working. The Germans tried to set up a makeshift defense waiting for the tanks. But the civilians didn't wait to see what would happen next. They came out of hiding and cheered the warning shots. The American army marched into Trabelsdorf. Vytas and his brothers watched and felt the excitement in the air. Everyone cheered and waved. Musicians began to play and the refugees and civilians danced in the streets with new energy.

"Vamoose!" they screamed at the German soldiers. The Germans walked away from their battle.

"Perhaps things will change, now," the boys said hopefully. They shouted loudly over the blaring brass bands.

"Does this mean the war is over? Did Russia lose? Who won?"

"Is it really over?" they asked.

"Not exactly," the American soldiers laughed. "It's close, but it's complicated."

Two American soldiers who spoke Lithuanian befriended Vytas and a couple of his friends. The soldiers invited the boys to meet with them at a *bierstuben.*

"This is a happy day for everyone. We're all glad you're here," Vytas said.

"Yes, it's a glad day for all of you... well for us, for Lithuanians. But for the Americans, not such a glad day."

"Why?" asked Vytas's friend. "Don't you want the war to end?"

"Of course," a soldier answered.

"It isn't that," another soldier said. "President Roosevelt died today. The very day we march into Trabelsdorf. He would have liked to have seen that." He emptied his glass, and wiped his eyes. A quiet pall settled over the Americans.

"That's too bad," Vytas said.

"Ja, so sorry," the others added.

They were deep into conversation past curfew when Vytas felt sleepy and decided to walk home. Walking down the middle of the street, he was surprised to hear a shout, "Halten!" He raised his hands in the air and stared into loaded rifles. He listened in German and answered in Lithuanian that he was on his way home to the farmer, and hadn't intended to miss curfew. The German gestapo followed him to the farmer's home.

"Is this your farm boy?" they asked.

"Ja." The patrol released him. The farmer scowled his disapproval at Vytas.

Nothing really changed much for 15 year-old Vytas and his family, even though the war was officially declared over only a few weeks later. World War II officially ended May 8, 1945, a day known as VE Day, Victory in Europe Day. The entire world rejoiced.

As the end of the summer neared, Vytas's family decided it was time to try to move into the American Zone. They rented a truck in the village to drive to Hanau, the displaced persons' camp near Frankfort.

This truck had been outfitted with a metal drum to act as a wood burning generator placed next to the engine. Gasoline for the cars and trucks was not available. The boys built a fire in the drum using blocks of wood. The truck moved slowly and frequently stopped. They poked the coals, and added more blocks of wood to keep the generator functioning. Driving slowly along an apple orchard, the boys riding in the truck bed yanked apples off the trees and dropped them into the truck bed at their feet. It was the first fresh fruit they'd had in a long time.

"Even the worms will taste good," Vytas teased.

When they finally reached the gate of the refugee camp in the American Zone, the guards wouldn't let them in.

"We don't know you. We don't know who you are. Maybe you are some of Hitler's Youth. Go away."

"Isn't this a refugee camp? Isn't this a displaced persons' camp?" Vytas asked.

"We are displaced Lithuanians. We're refugees," Vincus explained.

"So you are. The Nazis snatched boys like you off the street for their armies. Happened all the time; you might have been indoctrinated. We don't know; we can't risk that. You have no one who can vouch for you. You haven't documentation."

"But—

"Go away, you can't come in."

"I see someone," their father pointed out. "Let me call to that official over there. He knows us and can vouch for us."

One of the guards walked over to the official while the other continued to hold the family at gunpoint. The official accompanied the guard back to the truck and when he saw his old friend Jonas the bergenmmeister he grinned and stretched his hands toward him.

"Put your guns down," the official told the soldiers. He chuckled and pumped Jonas's hand. "I know this man. His family—displaced Lithuanians. A good man. Fine family. Let them in."

"Okay," the guard said. "We have to be careful, you understand?"

"Of course," Jonas said. "We understand that. And we appreciate the job you do."

The gate was opened and Vytas's family entered the displaced persons' camp. Vytas tossed the guard an apple and a smile.

Inside the camp, they saw confusion and chaos had followed them. The American military police surrounded the block that housed Ukrainians, Polish, and Russian refugees. They pushed, shoved, and hollered.

"I thought the war was over," Jon sneered.

"Looks like the start of the war all over again," Vytas whispered back.

"You have to return to your homes, now," the police shouted at the people. "Our government has deemed it is safe for you to return. The war is over. It's safe to go home."

The refugees argued yelling, "We are guaranteed death if we return home—

"We'll be sent to Siberia, you should know that."

"*Your* government doesn't know how it is. Americans don't understand what is really happening—

"That's right, and you don't understand Russia, either."

"You might trust Russia, you may think Russia an ally, but we know better!" the Lithuanians shouted angrily.

The MP's pleaded for cooperation. "Mrs. Roosevelt has a committee studying Human Rights. She says you will all be happy to be reunited to your homeland. It's best for everyone. We'll be returning you to your homes."

"You Americans still trust Russia, but we know better." The frantic voices got louder, more frightened, and more out of control.

"You may as well shoot us now."

"Mrs. Roosevelt? What does she know? How does she know what it's like in Poland for Polish people? She doesn't know, she doesn't understand. We can't return!"

The usually subdued refugees were hysterical. Men hollered, women argued, and children screamed. They ran away, hid, and hurled themselves out of the windows or into the river to escape going home. Many deliberately took their own lives. Vytas watched in silent horror. *The Americans are still allies with the Russians? Then who are our protectors? Is Mrs. Roosevelt for us or against us?*

Often in the evenings the Russian soldiers and politicians came into their camp. The refugees were forced to listen while the Russians promoted "going home." American MP's were assigned to protect the Russian speakers while they handed out their propaganda. The refugees begrudgingly snatched the fliers and listened politely. When the speech was over, they collected all the leaflets and literature and burned them in the street.

"Garbage. That's what it is. It's all garbage," the refugees complained.

"The Americans think the Russians are their friends. They will soon see," Vytas's father said.

"They blow with the wind. They are friends to no one. America will regret trusting them."

After several refugees ran away, some went missing, and others took their own lives, the government in Washington, D.C., sent an intelligence officer to investigate the camp. Lieutenant Colonel Albert Neil Cameron interviewed the refugees to figure out what they were afraid of. Why didn't they want to return to their homelands? He compiled a huge file, returned to Washington, and shared it with Mrs. Roosevelt and her committee. New policies were then put in place to help the displaced refugees and make immigration easier for them. They didn't have to return to their homelands, after all.

As displaced persons continued to file into Hanau, reports of relatives and neighbors were eagerly sought. Vytas learned his cousin Robert was missing. Robert's sister took her own life after being raped by Russian soldiers. His uncle, Robert's father, was arrested and shot. His aunt, Robert's mother, had gone to stay with his grandfather on their farm. He died two years after they left, and was buried in the Vepraia Cemetery. Most of the farm community of their Bergen, Vepraia, was gone, others informed him. Buildings were torn down or destroyed for the materials, and to force the farmers onto the collectives. Nothing remained on their family's vast acreage. The farmers who are still alive, he was told, now worked on the failed collectives and were starving.

Vytas stared at the dirty concrete walls. His jaw set, his eyes squinted, his fists tightened.

"Vytas. Come here, son."

Vytas shook himself alive and walked to his father.

"You must let go your anger, Vytas. God has spared us. Go outside and kick the wall. Then thank God you didn't break your toes. Anger saps your energy. You will need to be strong and energetic for what is to come. Anger and hatred will wear you down. Be strong. Thank God you are alive."

"Okay," answered Vytas shamefaced. "Okay. I can do it."

Chapter 28

Boy Scouts and Girl Scouts

"How is school in the refugee camp?" her mother asked.

"School is school," Danute answered indifferently. She didn't mind school, but she hated homework. There were so many other fun things she wanted to do instead. She wanted to do her chores, dance, play, read, and she made up all kinds of excuses to not get the school work done. Her school friends adored her fun-loving nature and before long the teachers all knew that Danute copied her friends' homework.

"Anyone who doesn't do his own homework will soon be caught because he won't know the material," the math teacher told the class, sending warning glances toward Danute. "You will punish yourself. Danute will now show us her work on the chalk board."

The girls giggled at the teacher's disappointment to see Danute put the work up completely and perfectly. She had an almost photographic memory. She remembered everything she copied, reading it just the one time. The teachers had to be satisfied that even though Danute copied the work, she also knew the material and passed her examinations. Long-legged Danute excelled in high jump and volleyball, earned satisfactory grades, and had many girlfriends.

Religion was a part of their school curriculum, as it had been all their lives. The students in the refugee camp were mostly Catholic; a few were Jewish. They had a quiet priest, a hidden church, a secret synagogue, an unknown rabbi.

"I wish I could have a new dress for Confirmation," complained Danute.

"Confirmation isn't about the clothes on the outside," her mother answered. "It's about what's inside you. Your aunt who is here in the camp will be your sponsor; the Bishop is coming. No new clothes."

Danute sighed. There was another reason she wanted to look nice that had nothing to do with Confirmation.

Danute and Vytas were among the large number of Boy Scouts and Girl Scouts in uniform who held troop meetings, classes in skills, took camping trips, and held dances while living in the refugee camp, pretending life was normal at this high school. They had several of the same friends and often ran into each other at social functions. Vytas was in the same Boy Scout Troop as Victor. To her annoyance, Danute felt an odd fascination with the tall, good looking Vytas. Catching a glimpse of him was enough to cause a brilliant blush to move up her neck and across her face. As disciplined as she was, she was unable to control her heart palpitations.

Vytas led the construction of a meeting facility for Boy Scouts in an abandoned horse barn, which was formerly a part of the German military. He scrounged for glass and putty to replace windows. He found a lot of brick, a result of the bombing, but mortar was almost as difficult to find as putty. He scrounged for the mortar and soon had a wall built at the entrance. He built decorations and fences from branches in the woods around the facility. He was a charismatic and natural leader. Danute was certain he'd never noticed her.

The troops went on camping trips. Some they hiked to, some required transportation, as with the trip to the Alps for the National Lithuanian Scout Jamboree. Dressed for the summer sunshine in their shorts, they were shocked when hail pelted their chapped red legs.

"It seems in the Alps it's winter even in the summertime," Vytas shivered.

Many of the Girl Scouts secretly paired off with the Boy Scouts and whispered about it later in their tents. Danute pretended she didn't care that Vytas paid her no attention.

"A boyfriend is the last thing I want," she said sternly.

In 1947, the Boy Scout World Jamboree was held near Paris. Eleven boys from Vytas's troop were selected to attend. Vytas and the other ten boys spent 30 days in the woods near the resettlement camp, to hone their skills, learn French, and prepare for the encampment.

The Russians said the Lithuanians could not go to the Jamboree as Lithuanians, they must go as Russians, since Lithuania was now part of the Union of Soviet Socialist Republic. They argued for weeks about whether to allow the boys to go. When the decision was made to allow the boys to go it was for their own political reasons. The boys didn't care; they were going. There was much joyful screaming and hollering as they packed their decorations, tables, and camp equipment. The Girl Scouts were happy for them and helped them to gather supplies. But, the boys couldn't represent their "former" country of Lithuania. It was a bitter pill to swallow. The Lithuanian, Latvian, and Estonian Boy Scouts were given a blue flag with a white clover leaf. None of the boys knew what it represented, but all Lithuanian, Latvian, and Estonian flags were destroyed, and the Boy Scouts were told they were representing Mother Russia as the USSR. The Scouts were happy to be going, but in their private meeting place they dared to show their anger at the injustice.

"Who knows what this flag represents?"

"Who cares? It doesn't matter. We know who we are, right?"

"But what is a USSR?" one of the younger boys wanted to know.

"We know our flag. This one is…well, what is it? A clover? What's that mean?"

"Who cares, anyway?"

"I've never seen it before. I think they just made it up."

"At least they aren't making us carry a *So-viet* ugly flag."

Vytas encouraged his troop to ignore the flag. "In our heart we are Lithuanian, or Latvian or Estonian, one and all. We will never be Russian."

"Yay," they cheered and whipped the new blue clover flag around disrespectfully. One boy pretended to wipe his nose on it. Another grabbed it and wiped it across the seat of his pants. Everyone laughed. Several boys sketched their true flag from memory and put the folded paper in their pocket. Their "real" flag would go to the Jamboree in their shorts pockets.

"USSR? What kind of made up name is that? Who will even know what it means?"

The boys marched with the strange flag bearing a clover and spent two weeks near Paris, visiting the Eiffel Tower, Notre Dame, and the Louvre. In Paris, flowers bloomed, fountains flowed, and grass grew in the parks. Busy people hurried in and out of shops. Paris, the Boy Scouts were surprised to discover, had apparently escaped the bombs.

"I thought the whole world got bombed," a young scout said. "Guess not."

Danute and her Girl Scout friends learned camping skills, took trips, and enjoyed learning other new skills. Her mother acquired parachute silk from the mill where she worked, and helped Danute sew a navy skirt and white blouse for her Scout project. She finally learned to sew. Learning to sew, and the proximity to the Boy Scouts, were two of the many good things about Girl Scouts from Danute's point of view. But, she and her mother continued to have differing viewpoints about many other things.

Chapter 29

Danute's Curfew

"I love to dance, Mama. But, why do I have a 10 o'clock curfew? No one else has to be in that early, why do I? Mother, you are so unreasonable. Please? Couldn't I just stay out a little longer? The dance is just getting going by ten. No one else has to leave, only me."

"Ten o'clock or not at all. Decent girls have no business out after ten."

"You could sneak in quietly when your mother is asleep," her friends whispered to her after class.

"It would never work with that huge loud clock in the middle of the town. She knows what time it is every hour when it chimes. Who doesn't? I hate that clock. They should have bombed it."

"That clock clangs so loud it wakes everyone in our house, too," her friend replied.

"My dad says he's going to shoot its face out one night," added another.

"Good," said Danute. "I wish he would. Ten o'clock. I just start having fun at ten o'clock; then I have to go home. It's so unfair. Unfair, unfair, unfair!"

At the next dance, Danute was having such a good time, she lost track of the time. She was laughing and dancing with a friend of her brother when the town clock bonged 11 times. She ran to her house. Her mother was asleep. Danute quietly slid into bed.

A few days later that boy was visiting her brother. They were talking about Scouts, school, dances, rules, curfews, and other favorite teen subjects, when Danute's mother uncharacteristically began to brag about her daughter.

"My Danute is always in at ten o'clock. She's a good girl, my Danute. I tell her 10 o'clock and she never misses. She's always in by ten. Always."

Danute felt her face redden. She cut her eyes to the boy.

Her jaw dropped in disbelief when he said, "Well, I don't know about that. I was dancing with her at 11 o'clock." Danute was furious at his betrayal. *Boys! Hmpf. Who needs them?*

Her mother didn't say anything, but Danute knew she was in deep trouble.

Later her mother said, "How dare you embarrass me, make a fool of me. You should be locked in your room. But, you have no room, and we have no lock. You shame me. You should be ashamed of yourself."

Danute continued to go to school and Scout dances with her group of friends, carefully watching her curfew hour. At the dances, couples wandered down "Lovers' Alley", a narrow path between the bombed out factories. Danute longed to walk with a boy, hold his hand, talk quietly. She secretly wished it could be Vytas.

"Vytas is tall enough even for you, Danute," her sister teased. "I know you like him."

"He's very cute," her girlfriends giggled.

"I see you blushing," one of them said squealed happily. "You look like you have Scarlet Fever. You must be in love."

"A lot you know," she retorted. "I'm not having any boyfriend. I'm going to be free and independent. I'll come and go whenever and wherever I want. I don't need a boyfriend or a husband. I might even be a nun. You don't know a thing about me."

"We think you have a crush on him," her friends whispered.

"If you didn't, you wouldn't care so much what we say," another said slyly.

"He's tall and good looking, too, mmm hmm."

"But, he's stuck up." Danute insisted. "And don't you dare tell him I like him. Because I don't." She'd never let him know that the sight of him at Scout meetings made her pulse race. *What if I let him know, and then he didn't like me? I couldn't stand it. It would be so embarrassing. I'd just die.* But, alone with her books and her thoughts, she often day dreamed of having a boyfriend, one who was taller than her. Someone who would walk with her down Lover's Alley and hold her hand. Someone who looked and talked like Vytas.

Chapter 30

Black Market

Vytas, a natural and enthusiastic leader, was often in charge of the Scout dances. He hired German bands to play for them and paid them with sandwiches.

"Why do you give our money and food to the Germans?" his friends asked angrily. "Why do we want to help them anyway?"

"Germans are also hungry," Vytas explained to his friends. "Haven't you seen? All of Hanau is leveled. Here at our camp, maybe only 10% bomb damage, but in their town, there is nothing left. And no work, either. No food. Nothing. Lots of kids have lost their dads. I feel sorry for them. The German people are also victims of Hitler. Not all of the Germans are our enemies. Not all Germans are Nazis. And, besides, it's a real good dance band, too!"

It gave his friends something to think about, but many weren't convinced and some decided to go to the movie instead of dancing to a German band.

There was one movie theatre outside town, about a mile walk. It was called Schloss, the German word for castle. It had formerly been someone's fine mansion. Few people had money for tickets. But Jonas worked in a warehouse, and Vincus worked in food distribution one time a week, so the family had some money coming in, enough for an occasional movie.

Vytas got his own money for the movies selling things on the black market. Because money was so scarce, people were often paid in merchandise, mainly cigarettes. Vytas sold his. Then he bought American scrip, tobacco, wine, chocolate, cognac, and sold that for a profit. He eventually made enough money to buy material for a fine suit.

"Someday in the future I will have a good job and I'll need some fine clothes," he explained.

"Hope you're right. About a future, I mean," said Jon.

The black market area, however, was not safe. His father warned him to stay away. But, for Vytas, it was the easiest way to make money. *Dad is always cautious. I'm big enough and smart enough. I can take care of myself.*

One night Vytas and his friends were on the way home when they decided to stop by the black market area and check out the action. It was deserted.

They were the only ones there. A car pulled in and slowed down. *A customer for the cigarettes in my pocket.* Vytas tugged the pack free from his pocket ready for a quick sale. *Oh, no.* It was the chief of police. One of the boys leaped over the fence and ran. The second was too scared to move. Vytas was too proud to jump the fence, so he stood tall and cooperated, ready to reap the consequences. The police took the two boys in. About an hour later one of the officials of the camp came to the police department to release the prisoners, and took them back to the camp.

Another time after he'd dropped off his date, he went by the black market area again to check on the activity. A jeep stopped beside him and the three strangers in the jeep asked for cognac.

"I have some. Wait here, I'll run home and get it." They pulled the jeep to the side and turned it off, waiting for Vytas to return. When he returned to the jeep the three men were leaning against the jeep.

Vytas heard, "One, two, three—

The first one hit him in the leg, the second one hit him in the forehead, probably aiming for the nose, and the third grabbed the cognac. They jumped into the jeep and took off.

Vytas told his friends about this mugging and theft and learned this was not the first time. The three in the jeep were regular thieves who had beaten up a number of boys, using the same scheme. Vytas and his friends laid a trap and turned the tables on the thieves.

With several of the biggest boys hidden, they set a smaller boy up as the bait. When the jeep appeared and asked for vodka, the boy said he'd be right back. When the three thieves got out of the jeep the mob set on them, three to one, and left them bruised and sorry by their jeep with flattened tires. It was the end of the thieving and muggings in the black market arena.

His mother and sister ended up in the hospital after eating fish from the black market and for a long time, none of the family would eat fish at all. Vytas had to agree with his father. The black market was dangerous in a lot of ways.

Chapter 31

Boyfriends and Girlfriends

Danute's friend Marita lived next door. She was Vytas's girlfriend. Because they had some of the same friends, same activities, used the same Scouting facility, attended the same school, Danute and Vytas occasionally spent time together in the same crowd of teenagers. They even traveled together on high school trips. Danute carefully kept her feelings to herself, but often felt the color rising hot on her fair complexion whenever Vytas was near. She ignored feelings of jealousy toward Marita, believing that to be a sin.

"Danute, why are you walking around with your eyes closed? You're just squeezing a little peek out of one eye. Why do you do that?" Marita asked.

"Shh. I'm just trying it. You know the girls all say if you meet a boy first thing in the morning before you see any girls, then it will be your lucky day. So

I'm just not looking until a boy comes by, then he'll be my first one seen. And I'll be lucky all day, maybe lucky in love."

"What! You're being so silly, Danute. It's a waste of your time anyway. You know your mother is going to fix you up. Why do you care about luck? Lithuanian girls don't have luck they have mothers. Your mother will find your man."

"My mother is *not* going to fix me up. If there's any fixing to do it will be my own, thank you."

"So you say. But we all know about our Lithuanian mothers, don't we? You might as well give up, Danute. Did you hear that Janie is marrying Vytas's brother Vincus? They will have a wedding here in the camp. I'll bet her mother had something to say about that, don't you?"

"That's old fashioned. And I'm modern." Danute changed the subject.

"Marita, I have a new dress from a cousin in America. You would like it, I think. Do you want to see it?" Danute unrolled the handed down, not-quite-but-almost-new, blue taffeta dress with a lace collar and a hint of cologne. She kept it rolled in a tissue paper to keep in nice.

"Oh, Danute, it's so pretty!" Danute smiled at Marita's sincerity.

"You can borrow it for a date sometime, if you want."

"May I? Really? This weekend?"

Danute loaned her new dress, wishing it were she going to Schloss with Vytas instead of Marita. Later when she reminded Marita to return it, Marita replied, "But, you never have any dates, you haven't got a boyfriend. Why do you need it? I need it. I need it more than you. You should let me have it." Danute gave Marita her cherished dress.

Marita and Danute stayed friends and shared many secrets, but Danute never let on about her crush on Vytas, and Marita never suspected. She boasted to their friends about how close she and Danute were and how they told each other everything. They'd be best friends forever.

"Someday when all this is over and we go home, we'll stroll our baby's carriages together through the park," she sighed wistfully. Danute rolled her eyes and changed the subject. Danute wondered if Vytas might notice her if she wore a blue taffeta dress with a lace collar and a hint of fragrance.

On a class trip to Cologne, the students gazed upward at the spires of the Cathedral of Cologne. The spires, second tallest of any church in the world, still reached to the heaven after taking 70 hits by aerial bombs. The stained glass windows still glimmered in the sunshine, completely intact. The city of Cologne surrounding the Cathedral lay in flattened ruins.

Some students crossed themselves; some spat on the ground rubble. Most were quiet while taking in the devastation and the amazing Cathedral left standing in its midst. Danute was stunned. *How could this be? Surely God had a hand in this.* Other students mimicked her thoughts.

"It's rumored that the allies used her spires to guide their bombing missions," one boy said.

"It's so beautiful," Danute whispered to Marita. "I can hardly take it all in."

Behind them, Vytas replied. "It's well built, that's for sure; strong structure, good masonry."

"He's so practical," Marita whispered to Danute. Marita swooned with awe.

"Hmpf," Danute said. "He's just trying to impress you." She glanced over her shoulder and caught Vytas looking at her, smiling. Her face blazed.

A trip floating down the Rhine with classmates was an occasion to forget the bombs, not look at the ruination of centuries of buildings, a chance to escape the homesickness and the turmoil in their young souls. It was a rare day of laughter and good times when the teenagers' faces looked young again. The deep furrowed worry lines were gone for today, washed in the cold, fast froth of the Rhine River. Danute felt so alive, so refreshed. With her face upturned to the sun, the wind whipped wisps of blonde hair across her cheeks. She closed her eyes and inhaled the clean fresh air.

"Having a good time, Danute?"

Startled, she turned and faced Vytas. Overcome by the blush, she could only nod and gulp.

"Yes. Yes, it's a grand day, isn't it."

Danute 1949

Chapter 32

CARE Packages

"Mother, look, another CARE package has arrived." Danute dropped the box on the floor and they pried the ends open. Across the front of the box in block letters it said *CARE United States of America.*

"Tell me again, Danute, what does the box say?" Danute pointed and recited each word carefully.

"CARE. Say it, Mother. K-K…"

"Why do I have to say it? You can do that, ja?"

"Ja. Sure. But you can learn to read the English words, too. I hope there will be chocolates in this one. I can sell chocolates for a good price and have money to give Kent to help with his college expenses. Chocolates sell easily."

"I know Kent appreciates his sister's help. But, do you know about this, Danute? Kent met an American priest, or maybe he was a bishop or a monsignor, I don't know. The man was an American traveling through Europe, though God knows why he'd care to do that these days. Such a mess in Europe. He's pastor of St. Joseph's Church in Connetty-cut in Amer-i-ca. Kent talks pretty good English and he says to the man, 'I have an uncle priest in Connetty-cutt,' and Danute, guess what? He knows him; he knows your uncle. Can you believe such a thing?"

"Really, Mother? But America is a big place."

"Ja, but I think Connetty-cut is a small place. I don't know. Anyway, Kent sent his address back to Amer-i-ca with the priest and said to have his uncle write to him at college in Kosova. And what do you think happened? Kent got a letter and a Fifty American Dollar from his uncle. Ja! Fifty dollar! Think of it."

"Fifty dollars? Well, I think we'll just eat the chocolates."

The mangled box finally surrendered and lay opened. Inside were seven smaller boxes along with some bags marked "macaroni," "cornmeal," "Carnation powdered milk."

"There's no chocolates, anyway," sighed Danute.

It wasn't long after that when an American-Lithuanian paid a visit to the camp. He was looking for Danute's family.

"I'm a neighbor to your uncle in Watertown, Connecticut. I'm visiting in Europe. I've brought you something." He handed her father an important looking packet of papers. He indicated a box beside him. "And I think this would be for your children."

Danute, Ilona and Victor went after the box like a belated Christmas morning. Inside was hand-me-down clothing from their cousins in America. Danute immediately checked all the pockets. One time when a package arrived from Lowell, Massachusetts, she found a dollar in a pocket. She sent the family a thank you letter, and checked pockets ever since.

"Look at this jacket," cried Victor. "No holes, and it even has all the buttons."

"And a skirt and a blouse. It's my size." Ilona ran off to try it on.

"This is so nice," cooed Danute. "Look, Mama, it has pleats all around. It's woolen, and it looks...new. Oh, I hope it will fit." She looked at her long legs and crossed her fingers. "I hope."

"The paperwork is all here," said her father at supper. "It guarantees the children will be schooled and we will have work. We have to have health certifications, then we just wait and see."

"Are we really going to America, Father?"

"What will we do there?" Ilona worried.

"I know what I'm going to do. I'm going to dance to Glen Miller and have Hershey Bars for breakfast!" Danute hopped up and twirled around her chair gleefully.

"Really, Danute, doesn't it scare you? I mean, who will you marry there?" asked Ilona.

"That's the least of my plans, I don't care. Maybe I'll marry an American movie star." She struck a seductive pose.

"Danute, that will do," her mother said sharply. "There are plenty of Lithuanians in America, Ilona. Don't worry about it, I'll find you one. Just think of being warm, with full stomachs, decent clothing, and a job, and money, and church, and— Anele hurried from the table, her hands over her face, overwhelmed by the possibilities.

"Please pass the gravy," their father said.

"Gravy? What gravy?" Victor quickly sorted through the table setting.

"The gravy we will have with every meal in Am-er-i-ca," his father laughed.

Chapter 33

Going to America

The family showed up at the clinic for their health evaluations, arriving early for their appointments.

"Let them see how reliable we are," said Anele. She was surprised to find the examinations so complete and thorough.

"Sure," said Victor with annoyance. "It's okay if we have bugs and be sick here, but we won't be allowed to take any bugs or sickness to Connecticut. That's what this is about."

"Danute, you need to stand very straight. Pink up your cheeks." She pinched Danute's cheeks.

"Ow! That hurt."

"Good, keep rubbing. Look pink; look healthy. Clear your throat. If they think you have TB we're done. And don't talk about how sickly you've been or your fainting spells in church. It's nothing. You finally got your period this year, fifteen, so late, you are finally maturing now, you won't be fainting anymore. Promise me."

Following the examinations the doctor said, "I find only two questionables in your family. Overall, this is a surprisingly healthy family. Danute has a few nits in her hair, and a slight heart problem."

"We will get the hair taken care of tonight." Her mother shuddered at the thought. "My husband is a pharmacist. He will look after anything else. There's nothing wrong with her heart, she's just growing very fast this year. Three inches in one year. And," she whispered, "menses."

"Ah," the doctor said knowingly, "that explains it. Well, get the nits out; I trust you'll do that. Your husband will know the right medicine for that. I'll sign all your documents now." He read, signed, notorized the papers, and handed them back. He winked at Danute, who responded with a crimson flush.

With the packet in his hand, her father looked pale, stunned, perhaps. Anele looked as if she would be the one to faint. Her relief nearly overwhelmed her. When they got home she went to work on Danute's scalp.

"Mother, leave some skin on my head," Danute wailed.

"Pew," said Ilona. "That stuff smells so bad, the bugs will run off your head and out the door to hide."

A half a year later, the family was finally packing. Or, at least they would have packed if they'd had anything left to pack. Danute had two tattered dresses, both hand-me-downs, and the pleated skirt she wore most days. She and Victor did both have new shoes made by a shoemaker. Sturdy, solid, brown leather shoes that were made to last. They were both proud to have a new pair of shoes, and they took good care of them.

On a biting windy day they left their immigration camp and moved to a dispersion point near the pier where they'd wait another week for their scheduled departure.

The family walked head down into the wind, up the eingang, into the *SS Marine Shark*. Had they been leaving their beloved country of Lithuania, it would have been a sorrowful occasion. But that had happened long ago. The country they were leaving now was not their home, nor were they sorrowful to leave Germany. On February 17, 1949, in Bremerhaven, Germany, they set sail for their new home in America.

"What will it be like?" Danute wondered aloud to no one in particular.

Chapter 34

USS Marine Shark

"It's so beautiful." Danute craned her neck trying to see everything at once. High ceilings, chandeliers, white tablecloths, she didn't know where to begin on this ship, the *SS Marine Shark*. There weren't many Lithuanians on board, but there were lots of Jews, and some Yugoslavians. Danute didn't care who was or wasn't onboard; she felt like Queen of all the World when the Captain's assistant bowed and kissed her hand. He was the nephew of General George Marshall, a name well-known to the refugees.

Once again the men and women were separated. Her mother was not happy.

"They are determined to destroy families," she stormed. "We have nothing but each other, and they always want to take that, too." Anele and Ilona were soon in bed anyway, green with seasickness. Danute was slightly nauseated, off and on, but determined no one would know. Her father and brothers were not sick, so she wouldn't be either. There were four people to a room, sleeping in bunks. Danute shared the room with her mother and sister, and a nice Lithuanian woman.

When the friendly waiters in white coats served them American meat on fancy plates and white tablecloths, Danute asked aloud, "Am I in heaven or something?"

After ten days of rolling on stormy seas, the *SS Marine Shark* docked at a pier in New York City. Her mother and sister had spent most of the ten days sick in their beds.

When dawn broke every passenger was standing on deck staring at the huge statue near the ship.

"I've seen the picture of this statue lady," whispered Danute to Ilona. "It's a symbol for America, I think."

"It's lovely," sighed Ilona.

"Ja. Ja, it is. It's so huge. I think that's like America, too. She has a crown, see? She's rich, like a queen. An American queen, sort of."

"She's Lady Liberty," a man told them. "She's welcoming us. Good luck to you."

The pier was crowded, but no one was talking much. They were looking. Looking for signage they could decipher, or people they might know, looking at the statue, looking for missing family members; looking for anything that looked familiar, while holding tightly to each other's hands and their small tattered suitcases.

"No one knows what to do next," Danute observed. She stood on one leg, then the other.

They stood in the long line and when it was finally their turn, Kent tried his English.

"We've nothing to declare," he said with confidence at the customs counter.

His mother patted his shoulder. "Good. Good English talking, Kent."

An uncle they'd not met before and his widowed sister-in-law were the greeting committee for Danute's family. Exhausted from the trip, Danute's mother was further weakened by her ten days of sea sickness. The family mustered a second wind to show gratitude to their American family who was taking them for their first meal in America.

Inside the restaurant, the American cousin chatted with Danute and learned of her heart's desire to own a pair of nylons with fancy seams down the back. She believed she'd look truly American when she could earn enough money to buy a pair of nylons, she told her cousin. The cousin was wearing a pair. Before the waiter brought their orders the cousin hurried Danute to the store next door and bought her a pair of nylons.

"You need to call yourself Donna. It's more American," the cousin suggested. Danute tucked the little package of dear nylon stockings into her coat pocket and Donna and her cousin returned to the restaurant.

Following dessert the exhausted family climbed into the commuter train to Waterbury, Connecticut. When they stepped off the train in Waterbury, they were greeted with a large sign hung in their honor: *Welcome HOME.* Danute stared in wonderment. The sign seemed to be giving off an aura of warmth, love, and safety. She was tired. She was safe. She was happy.

"What do the words say, Danute?" her mother whispered into her ear. "What do the American words mean? It's something nice, ja?"

"Ja, Mama. It's something very nice."

Vytas 1949

Chapter 35

"Nothing to Declare"

"Okay, then. It's time now. I told you, God would tell us when. Here it is; our document package." Jonas held the package up for the family to see. "In two days we will go to Budzbach for health screenings. Then…whatever it is that happens next."

The family was quiet. They stared at the packet in their father's hand. That packet would mark big changes for them all, changes they couldn't imagine. Vincus and his new wife Janie had already done this and were somewhere in the United States. None of them said it aloud, but they wished they would hear something from them. *How is it over there? What's it like?*

By the time they left for the health screening, they were all very excited and had convinced themselves the changes would all be wonderful.

They saw the doctors, dentists, psychiatrists, got shots, checked for lice, TB, mouth disease, and sanity. With all their forms filled out, signed, notarized, and in their hands, they headed back to Hanau, two hours by train.

Two weeks later, Vytas's family was loaded into a U.S. Army truck for their ride to Bremerhaven where they'd wait for their ship to come in. They stayed in a former military camp, similar to where they'd lived for the last few years. They made a trip into town to spend all their German Deutch Marks and chattered nervously about their upcoming adventure.

"Do you think four years of high school English will help us any?" Vytas asked.

"I doubt it," answered Jane. "I studied hard and got good grades, but when I listen to the American soldiers talking to each other, I don't know what they are saying."

"Ja, I thought so, too," added Jon. "The soldiers speak different than what we learned in school. I wonder how Vincus is doing?"

"It will be good to learn about the automobiles, though, ja, Jon? Did you find Flint, Michigan, on the map when you went in town?"

"I didn't find Michigan anything on the map. It was only New York on the map. I guess if you go to

New York you can find every place else from there. But, I'm ready to be an auto worker in Flint, Michigan. I'll work hard."

"Me too," the others chimed in. *Will the ship ever arrive?*

The *SS Mercy* slid into her berth at Bremerhaven a few days later. She was a hospital ship. The family got in the long line with their small suitcases and boarded. It was a tight ship. They slept in hammocks in tiers of three.

In spite of the good sailing weather, many passengers were so sea sick they couldn't show up for meals. Vytas found that to be an advantage as they were invited into the mess hall to eat all they wanted. There was always plenty of food left over.

Vytas and his ship board friend, a boy his age, were given official arm bands to be ship police. They patrolled at night with the ship guards. He practiced his English while chatting with the guards, sailors, and crew. It took six days to cross and on July 18, 1949, they dropped anchor in New York harbor, near the Statue of Liberty. Vytas watched the statue throughout the night, his heart hammering. They docked in the morning.

"Nothing to declare," they each said with practiced dignity. After navigating through customs and immigration, an official explained to them that their itinerary had been changed. They were not going to Flint, Michigan, after all. All the autoworker jobs had been filled. Instead, they were going to Omaha, Nebraska. Vytas and Jon studied the US map on the immigration office wall.

"It's a long way to go to Omaha, Nebraska," Jon whined.

"Just another train ride," sneered Vytas. "But, I think that's where the Indian Territory is. It might be dangerous. I saw it in a movie. Ja, Indian Country. Nebraska." The official put them on a streetcar to go to the train station. There the officials gave each one $2.00 and put them on the train to Chicago. They signed a document saying they would pay back the cost of their tickets when they got jobs.

"What do you think it will be like, Vytas?"

"I can't even imagine it, Jon. I hope there won't be Indians. That could be bad, I think."

Chapter 36

American Worker

When they pulled into Union Station in Chicago, Vytas and his family changed trains. During their layover, Vytas spent his last $1.25 in the station cafeteria. That would have to hold him until they reached Omaha.

Back on the train, Vytas watched the landscape changing as the train moved steadily westward, and kept his eyes peeled for Indians on horseback. Tired, hungry, uncertain of their destiny, the family was relieved to finally hear their station announced, "O-m-a-haaa, Omaha, Neb-rask-aaa."

Pulling their small suitcases from the overhead rack, they started down the aisle to the door. They stared into the wide open vastness of Nebraska. Overhead, an intense blue sky surrounded them. The warm wind blew into their faces. The smell of grain wafted on the wind.

It looks...smells...feels...a little familiar, Vytas thought. *Can Nebraska be like Lithuania?* He hesitated at the doorway. *Smells like home.*

"You looking for your Indians?" Jon teased. "Come on, Vytas, move."

"Hallo, there, hallo. Are you Jonas and family?" It was a jovial priest stretching his hand out to their dad and speaking Lithuanian.

"Ja, it's us," Jonas said, extending his hand. "I am Jonas; this is my family. Only we don't know why we are here at Omaha, Nebraska."

"I'm Father Joseph. Welcome to Omaha, Nebraska, USA. I'm pastor at St. Anthony's Catholic Church in Omaha. We have a nice church, nice Lithuanian church, but many parishioners are moving away, getting new jobs, and going to California. I told the immigration committee, 'you have more Lithuanians coming? You send them to me. I will see they have homes and jobs.' Build St. Anthony's back up, too," he smiled. "Helps everybody."

"We can work, ja. We'd like jobs. We are farmers. We're used to hard work." Jonas introduced the rest of the exhausted family to the priest. "This is my wife, Sofie, my daughters Jane, Irena, Dona, my sons Jonas, called Jon, and Vytas. My oldest son Vincus married and immigrated before us. He's already in America."

"How do you do, so nice to meet you all. I know you'll be happy here, and St. Anthony's will be happy to have you. These are some of our parishioners, here to welcome you." The strangers shook hands with each family member, bussed the cheeks of the women, and picked up their suitcases.

Pastor Joseph chatted amiably about the nice house he had for them to live in and the farm where they would work. Jon struggled to keep his eyes open; Vytas yawned and leaned against the pillar in the station. His mother and sister dawdled behind, stumbling through a fog of exhaustion and hunger.

They were all relieved when the priest said they would stop at a restaurant and he would buy them supper before driving them to the farm. They were so tired, they barely remembered all he told them. Vytas was so sleepy he later couldn't remember what he ate at his first American meal.

"Here we are," Father Joseph said. "This farm is owned by a doctor who's invested in several farms and businesses in the area." The priest finally saw how tired the family looked.

"I'll come back tomorrow and show you around. You all need to test the beds now, I think," he chuckled. "Sleep well."

"I think I will sleep 100 years," groaned Vytas.

The priest, true to his word, showed up after breakfast to tour them around the farm.

"It's a nice house," they all told the priest. "Very nice for us."

"This farm is situated on the high bank of the Elkhorn River." He pointed at the horizon. They walked a fair distance from the house and viewed the beautiful river flowing through the farm property.

"The Elkhorn joins the Platte River a few miles downstream. Have you heard of the Platte River? It's a big river. Maybe famous, at least here in Nebraska." They toured the fields, the barns, and the out buildings. Vytas looked over the tractor and the farming implements.

"I know how to drive and use these," he assured the priest.

"Might as well get at it," Jane said. She rolled up her blouse sleeves. Her mother tied a scarf around her hair. Vytas smiled. *Just like home.*

"Let's get to work," Jonas said. *Ja, just like home.*

The house they lived in was three miles from the farm fields. Every day Vytas drove the tractor and his father and brother rode in the trailer to and from their work.

Eventually Vytas and Jon saved enough money to buy a 1941 Ford with their combined savings.

Donna 1950s

Chapter 37

Connecticut

Over breakfast coffee, decisions were made as to housing for the family of six.

"Ilona must go to school," the cousin said. "We will help with her tuition and get her a room there. It's a fine Catholic Girl's School. She will make friends and be happy there."

Danute overheard these remarks and wondered if anyone had asked Ilona if she wanted to go to a boarding school away from her family.

"What will I be doing, then?" she asked.

"We'd like you to go to Watertown. Uncle's daughter is expecting a baby and she already has a toddler. She needs some help. Will you work for her?"

She smiled and nodded. *There's not any way to say no to these kind people. And what other plan do I have?* Kent found work and then a place of his own. Victor stayed with their parents in Waterbury. Within a couple of weeks both her brothers found jobs. Kent worked in a factory and went to college nights. Victor went to New York State College School of Cooking.

Their father, who'd been a pharmacist and army officer, worked at Taft School as a dishwasher, making $72.00 a week. He had a room there and came home on weekends. The family was safe, comfortable, and paying their way. But mother Anele wanted the family together. She was not happy.

She found a small apartment in Union City near her husband's work and planned to move her family.

"Now we are no one's responsibility," she said. "We have our own place, we are all working, we pay our own way, and we are all together again." The family knew that was the most important thing to their mother. They furnished the apartment with household items found at bargain basement sales. Their uncle gave Kent money to buy a decent used car. Their father moved in, and their mother was happy again.

The family looked forward to Sundays and Mass at St. Joseph's in the Waterbury, Connecticut suburb called "Brooklyn," a typical turn-of-the-century ethnic neighborhood with Lithuanian stores, restaurants, and church. At the beginning of every week, they all got a dose of familiarity at Mass, speaking Lithuanian and Latin.

A neighbor of the cousin owned a Laundromat and asked Danute to come to iron for her at 50 cents an hour. Danute was thrilled. Now she'd have her own money. She'd even be able to go to the movies. Her first American film, paid for with her own money, was a Lou Costello movie. She wore her stockings, paid her own admission, and laughed when the Americans laughed. She felt very American. The next thing to go were the brown oxfords, traded for a new pair of American-looking shoes to wear with her nylon stockings.

"Danute, hurry up, someone waiting to see you," her mother greeted her at the door.

"Hello, Pastor," she said.

"Danute, bless you. My sister who lives in New Haven has been injured in an accident. I need to find someone to help her out. I wonder if you would consider this job?"

"Of course."

She moved to New Haven, next door to the Yale University boys' dormitory. The second story window of the dorm faced the second story bedroom window of her room.

"My friends will all be so jealous," she giggled as she waved hello through the window at interested Yale boys.

The difficulty for Danute was her injured patient couldn't sleep nights and insisted Danute stay up with her and play canasta. While the patient slept in the daytime, Danute was working. She found herself falling asleep whenever she sat down. She tried to stay awake on football days so she could watch the boys in their streaked fur coats with their girlfriends on their arms. Such excitement she thought. *Sometime I must find a way to go to a football game and see this good time for myself.*

Downstairs on the street level of their building, a Greek family ran a restaurant that served dinner and breakfast. Before long they were asking Danute to help there, too.

"Come, Sunshine, and work with us. We like to have you around, you are so much fun. Everyone likes having you around, and our customers like you, too. We'll all help you learn English. You can fill the salt and pepper and sugar bowls. We'll pay you."

"Okay," she agreed, as her new friends sang "You Are My Sunshine" in her honor.

They insisted she was too skinny and fed her desserts constantly. They doted on her and made it their project to Americanize her. Her new friends played with her hair and gave her lipsticks. They all called her Sunshine. She soon figured out it was a novelty to have a foreigner around for their amusement.

When Kent came to visit her he put on his big brother role.

"Lipstick! Why are you wearing lipstick? Father will not be happy about that. You look, you look, like…I don't know, but not like Danute. Like…like American. You think you are a film star? Wipe it off." He reported his sister's errant behavior to the home front.

Her father wasn't happy that Danute was "changing." He wanted her forever his little girl.

"Lipstick? Stockings? What will you do next? Change your name to Donna to be more American?" So when a friend of her cousin asked to hire her to be a nanny for her children, to live with them, Donna's family nixed it. They didn't want her to be gone from them they told her. But Danute knew it was because they feared her living with Americans, and becoming more like Americans.

"See this, Danute? I too can be American," her father joked. He had bought a TV. This was a new and exciting invention that took up a great deal of space in their small apartment. The wide wooden box with the small green window took half the wall. When the television wasn't on, they used the window for a mirror. They watched the six o'clock news every day. Danute's favorite program was Milton Berle's Show.

"Time now for Uncle Miltie," she announced. She fixed her plate of food and carried it from the kitchen to eat in front of the TV. Her father smacked the kitchen table with the palm of his hand.

"This is what they do in America? They don't eat at the table with their family? In this house we will eat together. I don't like this. I'm losing my children. It scares me, Anele. I don't like all this change."

"Danute, come back to the table, now. We eat together," her mother said. "You heard your father."

"Dad, this is how it is. We're not in Lithuania. It's not 1930s. We're in America. It's 1950s. Lots of things are changing. We need to change, too."

"We live here, but we are always Lithuanian, and we have our own ways. Don't forget it."

Chapter 38

Changes

For Danute, learning to change and adapt, meant giving up some of the "truths" she'd grown up with.

"Really? There is a dance *this* weekend? But, it's Advent," Danute said with surprise.

"Right. So?"

"But there's no music during Advent. It's a quiet time of preparation for the birth of the Christ child. No celebration, not yet. Just contemplation. No music, no dancing. Not until Christmas, when Advent is over."

"Really? I never heard that before. Maybe it's a Lithuanian tradition," her girlfriend said.

"Ja, I guess so, in America music seems to be a part of Advent. I hear Christmas music in the stores and on my radio. Christmas music, when it isn't yet

Christmas? Christmas dances during Advent season? I don't know. I've never done that. I really like to dance. I'll have to think about it. I'll let you know."

Should I go? Should I sing? Dance? Isn't it a church rule? No music during Advent. Is it a Catholic rule? Or is it only a Lithuanian custom? What should I do? Maybe it's the American's who are wrong about this one. Or maybe...not. Shall I accept the invitation? How uncomfortable will I be? Can I forget for the evening that it's Advent? I don't know what to do.

Two teachers lived below their aunt and had helped Danute with school, when she went to New Haven High School in the evenings for a year. But they couldn't advise her. She talked to her priest and went regularly to confession. She asked his guidance. But, only she could come to grips with what changes she wanted to make, and what changes she couldn't, or wouldn't, accept.

Ilona graduated from the Catholic Girl's School after two years, but before she could get a job she developed TB, went into the hospital, and returned to Waterbury. Their mother's health wasn't good either, and it seemed to be understood that Danute would care for her sister and her mother.

Danute's internal turmoil began to turn outward. She blamed everyone for her sister's TB. She'd never been close to her mother, but she did empathize with her bad health and understood that her mother wasn't able to look after sick Ilona. But,

Danute didn't want to take on the care of her sister and her mother. *When can I live my own life? In Lithuania I wouldn't have a choice. It would be my family obligation. Is it still my obligation here? What about my obligation to myself? I have so much to see and try in America. It's all new and exciting. I don't want to stay home. Is that selfish? Am I selfish? God, forgive me, if I am.*

"The TB sanitarium is a beautiful new facility in Middlebury. Why can't she stay there?" Danute asked the family.

"Why should she stay there when you can take care of her here just fine?" her mother retorted.

Will I always be the one they will call on to help? Maybe that's what I should change. Or maybe that's what I'll have to accept. Guilt ate away at her. Her enthusiasm for her new life in America ebbed, and she sagged into depression.

Kent suggested she get a steady job in a factory, and take a correspondence course.

"Get out some," he said. "Learn a trade. Make your own way. Then you'll feel more like your real self."

God bless him. I think he understands how I feel.

She found work in a glass company where she earned 50 cents an hour cleaning glass. The thin sheets of glass were cut, then cleaned, fired and bent to make the decorative glass balls on gasoline pumps, faces of clocks, and curved picture frames. She took her job seriously. This was a small company, very private, and close to home. *Just right for us Lithuanian kids*, she thought bitterly. *Not too far from the apron strings.* Her depression returned. She needed more money if she would ever manage to be on her own. She applied at the U.S. Rubber Company where they made gym shoes. But she had to be a U.S. citizen to work there. It would be five more years before she could get a job there.

She filled out applications and registrations best she could, mailed them in to a correspondence school, and began her studies in accounting. Kent cheered her on. It was their secret.

Chapter 39

Citizen Donna

She and Ilona applied for citizenship as soon as they were eligible. Their uncle's secretary went with them to Waterbury, Connecticut, for their interview. The three women chattered nervously all the way to Waterbury testing each other on every possible question they might be asked.

"I think I know as much about this government as the women who have lived here all their lives," Danute said. "I've learned the booklet by heart."

"I know," said Ilona. "My teachers don't even know all the answers about their own representatives. But I can list them in my sleep."

They slid into the long line of immigrants trodding nervously up to the second floor for their interviews. Danute noticed some were perspiring, some were twisting handkerchiefs. One had bit her lip and was dabbing the blood with a Kleenex. A man fingered his mustache. Observing the women in sturdy practical shoes, wearing babushkas on their heads, and the men with their hats in their hands, Danute recognized herself as a "typical immigrant."

As the group made their way up the stairs, carefully keeping to the right, two young American lawyers in expensive suits and shiny shoes rushed down the steps toward them. A pungent trail of Old Spice followed in their wake.

"The first one said derisively, "What have we got here?"

"Just a bunch of green horns," the other answered without so much as a glance their way. Danute snorted in a quick gasp of stale air. The remark stung like acid; her eyes teared. She was glad Ilona hadn't been paying attention and had missed the cutting words.

When it was finally their turn, Danute tugged on Ilona's arm as her sister headed into the office.

"Just do the best you know; don't worry," she advised. "I'll be praying for you."

In a short few minutes Ilona came out smiling.

"You are finished already? Why are you—

Danute was immediately called. She stood and went into the office, still puzzled at how quickly Ilona had returned.

The official sat across from Danute at a wide desk, fountain pen in hand, open ink bottle sitting on the blotter in front of him.

"Sit down. You are?"

She told him her name and he checked it off the lengthy list in the ledger. He looked bored. Her heart hammered.

"Can you speak English?" he asked gruffly.

"Ja. Yes, I mean, yes. I speak English okay."

"Can you understand English when it's spoken to you?"

"Yes. I do understand."

"Okay, you may leave. Next."

She stood on weak knees and made her way to the door. Her sister and the secretary stood grinning.

"It's over," her uncle's secretary said with a shrug of her shoulders.

"But, the questions? I know the answers. Doesn't he need to know how much I know?"

"Too many people, not enough time," the secretary said. "Let's have lunch to celebrate and go home. Congratulations, ladies, you're soon to be American citizens."

When the time came for Danute's swearing in ceremony, she, Ilona, and 87 other immigrants stood before the judge, raised their right hands and pledged their loyalty to their new country. *Greenhorn. We'll see about that.*

Danute paid $10 to have her name changed officially from Danute to Donna.

"Father won't like that," Ilona warned her.

"He can still call me Danute. But, it's me who has to live my life, and I want to live it as Donna."

She worked on a conveyor belt in a factory with Polish women who had been in the United States for a while. When the work made her dizzy she fainted. The Polish women were kind to her and wanted her to do well. They were all paid "piece work," so when Donna felt dizzy or fainted, the women did their work and they did hers too, so she would still be paid. Her Lithuanian supervisor pretended not to notice.

"Everyone has been very kind to me. Thank you," she said sincerely.

She studied the Polish women who seemed to be mostly Americanized. She tried to discern what changes they'd accepted, and which they hadn't. She tried to mimic some of what they did, sort of trying it on for size, to decide if it was a comfortable change for her. She also copied some of the American speech she heard around the factory, on the train, and on the street. She noticed the slang and expletives and when she dropped something, she mimicked, "Osheet." The ladies laughed, and explained to her what she'd said was profanity. Donna felt her face heating up and knew it was red as a beet. This was one change she wouldn't make. Several Lithuanian words, Donna discovered, sounded like American profanity, and often sent her English speaking friends into fits of laughter while Donna and her Lithuanian companions looked at each other in confused embarrassment.

"I'm sorry," she said. "I never use profanities. I heard that someplace. I didn't know it was bad to say. Excuse me, please. I learned English in Germany. They didn't tell us everything." She visited the confessional and vowed to not use that word again.

After a couple years she was able to buy living room furniture and a TV for her own apartment. She also bought her long-desired first sewing machine, patterns and gabardine cloth. Now she could sew her own new clothes. She would be stylishly American. She visited her mother often and regularly, but not often enough to satisfy her mother who wanted her family all together all the time.

Chapter 40

Chicago

"Danute, I want you to come with me. I am one of the organizers of this grand national festival for 1955, a Lithuanian convention. I've worked very hard on this committee. Come with me to Chicago. We will stay in a fine hotel, ja? We will dance and have a good time," her father implored.

"This sounds like a fun time. Ja, I will come."

They stayed in a downtown hotel in Chicago. She saw a lot of friends from the camps in Germany, now all grown up like herself. It was really like a reunion, with food and music, dancing and hugs. Her mother's cousin visited Chicago, and Donna met other relatives for the first time. She suddenly felt she had many friends and relatives, and they all connected her to Lithuania, and to Chicago. She didn't feel so much like a fish out of water, as she had for the last few years. On the streetcar, she met an old friend from the German camp who was now a piano teacher in Chicago. They promised to stay in touch.

When the festival was over, she packed to go home, but her mind had been made up. She would return to Chicago.

"How can you do this to us? Is this how to treat your old parents? You children are so ungrateful. Your sister has met a boy, she says. I'm finding a husband for her and she's finding a *boy*. And now you want to leave? You are finding a *boy*, too? You are leaving to go to Chicago? You need to take care of your sister. How can you do this to me and your poor father? We are not young, you know." Her mother scolded and pouted.

Donna argued with her mother. "I've had my own place for a while now; I did fine on my own. I'm not a child, Mama, and neither is Ilona. I have my own money and a lot saved. It's not about a boy. I want to go to see the world in Chicago. Union Station, oh, Mama, you should see it; it's like another whole world. It doesn't mean I don't want to be your daughter."

"Another whole world? Two worlds aren't enough for you already? Then you go. You've made up your stubborn mind anyway. But, if you go, I will disown you. So you just decide yourself. My daughter – or not."

"That's not fair, Mama."

Rock and a Hard Place

Donna cried all the way to Chicago. She stowed her suitcase in a locker at Union Station and bought a newspaper. She had to find a job. *If I fail my mother will never let me forget it.* She took a room at The Girls' Club in Lincoln Park, complete with maid service and a roommate. She called her friends, and found a job using her accounting certificate from the correspondence school. *Kent was right about that. I will telephone him from the pay phone booth and say thank you.* She was hired as the bookkeeper, timekeeper, and overseer of insurance in charge of 200 people at Hart, Schaffner, and Marx, a men's clothier. She was an American citizen, free, and independent, supporting herself, far from Russia, far from Germany, and oh so far from Lithuania.

Vytas 1950s – 1980s

Chapter 41

Immigrant Perspective

Fifteen miles away from the farm in Omaha stood a rock quarry, carved out of the hillside, another of the doctor's investments. Vytas got a second job delivering rock at the end of the day. After a year and a half Vytas was driving tractors, dump trucks, and using all kinds of farming equipment. He had proven himself a capable and reliable worker. He was making 50 cents an hour. He asked for a raise to $1.00 an hour. The doctor agreed, but after a month, he rescinded the agreement saying he couldn't afford that much.

Jon left the farm after a year. Vytas and his father were unable to manage the sizeable farm alone, and Vytas wasn't happy with his wages. They'd heard about good paying jobs in the meat packing industry. The family decided to move from the farm.

Vytas got a job working at Cudahy Packing Company. This large company slaughtered, processed, and packed meat. Once they were settled in the city, Vytas bought a new 1951 Chevy.

"So, Vytas, you have a fancy, flashy new car, eh?" his American co-workers smirked.

"Not flashy. Just new," he answered. "The cheapest model available, but it's new, and ja-yes, it's mine."

"Where'd you get that kind of money?" one asked sourly.

"Immigrants get preferential treatment," another said slyly and quietly. Vytas felt their jealousy as much as heard it, and he was annoyed at their smugness.

"There was no preferential treatment. I save my money, that's all. I work hard, I save, that's the way to do. That's the way you get what you want. Maybe immigrants do that better because we know how easily we can lose everything. So we work hard, we don't squander, we save our money."

"What do you mean squander? We don't squander."

"Well, it depends. If you like to go to the restaurant and buy one meal for what I spend on food for the week, then you won't have so much to save even though we make the same wages."

The jealous co-workers shrugged uncomfortably. "We see you dancing at Peony Park, too."

"Yes, I go dancing. You buy drinks all evening long. I buy one 7-Up and sip it all night. You go both nights, I go once in a while. So, however much you spend Friday is how much I save. You could save enough to buy this car, too, if you would be frugal."

"But, sometimes I run out of money before my paycheck and I even have to borrow to get by," one complained. "I don't have any to save."

"I know you do. But, I always have money in my pocket. You need to make better choices how you spend your wages." He could see they weren't convinced. Even though they were jealous of his car, they weren't willing to make the sacrifices to save money.

"Credit, you know, that's the future of banking in this country." The cocky young man pushed his cap back to grin at Vytas. "Yep, that's the new way. It's going to make a difference in the economy."

"Maybe," said Vytas, "but it might not be a better difference."

Donna 1960's

Chapter 42

American Soldier

The Lithuanian community in Omaha and St. Anthony's Church was growing steadily, thanks to the hospitality of Father Joseph. The community supported each other and welcomed new comers. Whenever new immigrants arrived, the priest gathered some of his flock to meet the train with him and welcome the newest members. Vytas often went along.

It was at the train station when he was 19 years old that Vytas first laid eyes on a 19 year-old tiny, shy, Lithuanian girl arriving from Chicago with her family. She was ordinary looking, poor, like the rest of them, but something about Aldona attracted his attention.

He invited her to the movies, and they went out with friends off and on. Peony Park, where the big bands came to play and people danced, was a favorite date night for most of the young people. Vytas and Aldona danced, took rides in the country, and fell in love. Everyone seemed pleased with the arrangement except Vincus.

"I don't understand you, Vincus. You got married when you wanted. Why don't you want me to marry Aldona? What is it about this marriage you don't like? You don't want me to be happy? You don't like Aldona for a sister-in-law? Why not? She's a fine girl. What is this about?"

"I don't want to talk about it. I just don't think you should do this. It's not the right thing, I think. You need to listen to me. Take my advice and call this off."

"No. Not until you can tell me what your objection is. You aren't making sense to me. There is no reason I shouldn't marry Aldona. If you know a reason, you should tell me. I'm going to marry her, Vincus."

Vincus walked away from his brother. They'd had this discussion a few times already. Still, Vytas didn't know why his brother didn't want him to marry Aldona, and it seemed he might never know.

In 1952, at age 22, Vytas married Aldona at St. Anthony's Church in Omaha on a blistering hot June day. It was so hot, the traditional rain of rice stuck to the bride's and groom's faces. It was a humble, traditional, Catholic, Lithuanian wedding, with both their families, Vincus included, and some friends in attendance. The reception party was at the bride's home. It was so hot the floral decorations wilted and the ice cream melted. Vytas and Aldona only noticed each other.

Aldona worked at a crate factory and lived with her family in a spacious house. The newlyweds moved in with her family while they saved their money for a home of their own. In November, 1952, Vytas was drafted into the army. He kissed his young wife goodbye and boarded the Greyhound Bus for Fort Bragg, North Carolina.

One day while his unit was having maneuvers in the woods at Fort Bragg, Vytas was told to report to the commander's office. He jumped into the waiting jeep.

"What have I done now?" he asked. The driver shrugged. It wasn't his business to know. In the commander's office he was told which barrack he needed to report to for an interview.

"Yes, Sir," he saluted. He couldn't imagine what was in store for him next. *What kind of interview do I need? Am I in trouble?*

He reported to the barrack. A clerk with a clipboard checked the orders.

"Do you know what the three branches of government are?"

"Ja. Yes. Of course I do. Executive, Judicial, Legislative."

"Good, Soldier. Do you want to change your name?"

"What? I don't understand. What you are talking about."

"Becoming a U.S. Citizen. Do you want a different American name?"

"I haven't been here long enough to become a citizen."

"You're in the military. We waive the five-year waiting period. You're already serving this country. Wouldn't you rather do it as a citizen?"

"Sure. But my name? It's simple enough to say. No, I won't change that."

About 80 U.S. Army soldiers, all natives of other countries, stood on the bleachers on the parade grounds at Fort Bragg, North Carolina. Already serving their new country of America, they raised their right hands, swore their allegiance, and officially became citizens of the United States of America.

Chapter 43

Living the Dream

Two years later when Vytas was discharged, he and Aldona became disenchanted with Omaha. The job Vytas had prior to his service with the army wasn't the same job. There was friction at the packing company, talk of a strike. Aldona was unhappy with her pay at the box company as well. Risking all, they packed their few things and moved to Chicago.

Aldona found work at the Nabisco Company, and Vytas at International Harvester. Two weeks later, when International Harvester went on strike, he got a job at Rock Island Rail Road remodeling and repairing passenger cars. After two years when the railroad laid him off, he got occasional jobs cleaning churches and schools while waiting through the next year for a call from the railroad to return to work.

"Why do you that?" his friends asked. "Why work? Take it easy. Collect your unemployment. It's as good as a paycheck. Let the government take care of you."

"It's not up to the government to take care of me. That's not their job."

"Sure it is. They got the money. They got the power. Let them take care of us."

"Whose money do you think it is they have? You talk like a communist," Vytas grumbled.

"We're not commies, man, just collecting what's due to us. You know, all for one, one for all, that kind of thing."

"You want to get paid for breathing? You want the government to mind your business? The communists think this way. Everybody equal. You can get up and go to work or stay in bed, everybody gets paid the same, everybody equal? That's how the Socialists think. Be careful. It doesn't work. I've seen it."

"Sounds pretty good to me," the guy laughed.

"Bring it on!" laughed another. "What part doesn't work, Vytas?"

"When men don't work, they lose their ambition. Then, no initiative, no creativity. Soon no one wants to work. Why should you be ambitious if you'll never get ahead? Why work? Let the government take care of you, eh? I saw good productive farms owned by hardworking farmers made into government collectives, everyone sharing equally, paid by the government. The farms turned into sour wasteland. No one had anything. No one cared. Yes, then everyone is equal, that's for sure. Everyone is poor. No one has anything. You want money? Go to work."

"Aw, I don't know. Sounds like a good idea to me."

"If it was such a good idea, why are all us immigrants over here? We could all be home living a good life. Why do you think we're here?"

After a year, the call to go back to work at Rock Island Railroad still hadn't come. Vytas and Aldona lived frugally, while their American friends continued to live as if they had steady pay checks coming in.

"Just buy it on credit, Vytas. That's the way of the future. You think like an old man from the old world. The future of the country depends on us young men with modern ideas. Credit, that's the ticket. We'll show the world how it's done."

"You don't want to work, you buy things you can't afford on credit, then pay for them with someone else's money. Is this how you plan to show the world? What will happen when you run out of other people's money? If that's your modern idea, then good luck to all of us."

Through an acquaintance, Vytas was offered a job at the National Congress of PTA as the chief custodian of the huge, modern building. The Rock

Island Railroad still hadn't called him. He left the railroad, accepted the PTA job, and went to work.

Vytas and Aldona built a new house in a Lithuanian neighborhood where they lived the American dream for the next 15 years: jobs, a home, work, love, and peace surrounded by friends, neighbors, and family. They both found old acquaintances in Chicago from their days in the resettlement camps in Germany. They entertained, played cards, and enjoyed their new freedoms. They traveled the country during their vacations visiting most of the states and Canada, camping and fishing, until Vytas retired with a gold watch and a big party at age 60.

In the Chicago paper Vytas saw an ad that a Lithuanian couple was looking for a caretaker of their estate in Cashiers, North Carolina. They had 80 acres and would build the caretaker a house on the property. Vytas and Aldona made the trip to apply for the job, only to find the couple had changed their mind. But, after spending four autumn days in the beautiful Blue Ridge Mountains, the couple had discovered their retirement heaven.

Donna 1960s-1980s

Chapter 44

Single Girl's Dilemma

Independent Donna, a thoroughly modern city girl in Chicago, dated off and on. At the large international clothing store, Hart, Shaffner, and Marx, she managed the financial floor of 200 people. There were few Lithuanian men. Italian and Spanish men seemed to dominate the tailoring industry. Her Lithuanian friends had been friends of her mother, and they knew her mother was angry that she was here, so at first they were standoffish. But, Donna deferred to them as stand-in parents. Eventually she was invited into their homes and taken under their wings. They introduced her to some Lithuanian fellas, but Donna wasn't really interested in casual dating.

"What's the point?" she asked. "I want to get married. If a guy is interested in casual friendship, or in *other* arrangements that I'm definitely not interested in, why do I want to waste my time?" Her friends were exasperated. "Casual dating is like window shopping with no money. What's the point? I've got money and I want to invest."

"Donna, you are so square," her girlfriends said.

"Can't you loosen up a bit? Just have fun. What's wrong with dancing with a guy, or even kissing him, if he's good looking."

"Good looking doesn't mean he's somebody I want to kiss. If I kiss somebody, he's the one I'll kiss for life."

"You really are square, Donna. You don't know what you are missing."

"I know."

"Loosen up and have some fun. That's a really old-fashioned attitude, you know."

"Maybe," she said. "But I will call the shots in my life. And I will never do anything to bring shame to me or my family. If I let boys decide what I will do, or who I'll kiss, I might shame myself and my family. Is that square? I don't know, and I don't care. If that's old fashioned, that's how it is. I'll just be square and old fashioned. I'm an independent girl, and I'll make up my own mind about these things. It's too important to let anyone else decide for me."

"But, Donna, you're practically an old maid. Older men are interested in you. You might have to be a little…flexible, you know, not so square."

"Really, Donna, we aren't kids anymore, you know. We're already twenties! Older guys, well, maybe they expect, you know, not so square."

Donna felt the sting, the truth of that remark. Older men had asked her out. But she was afraid to go. She never trusted their intent. Her friends had no idea how many dates she'd turned down.

She went with friends to a Lithuanian celebration downtown. Crowds of people were dressed in traditional festive clothing, the national costumes of Lithuania. There was a colorful parade, lively music, food everywhere, and folk groups dancing. The air was wild with Lithuanian aromas and sounds.

"Danute!" Someone in bright costume grabbed her and hugged her. Donna studied her face, then smiled at her friend from camp in Germany.

"Katarina," Donna embraced her.

"Katie, now," Katarina said.

"Okay, yes, and now I'm Donna," she laughed.

"We have just got to get together," Katie said. "I have to go now, my group is dancing, but let's get together, and soon. It's wonderful to see you. This is Eddie. Eddie, this is my old favorite friend, Donna. We need to get together again."

He offered Donna his hand and shook hers. "We're going to the beach at Lake Michigan on Sunday. Why don't you come along, Donna?" The girls exchanged phone numbers and the laughing couple joined the throng of folk dancers. She tucked the paper in her bag and looked forward to Sunday.

Sunbaking on the white Lake Michigan sand, Katie dozed, read a book, swam, drank seltzer from bottles, and flirted with the guys on the beach. Donna sat on the blanket in the shade of an umbrella and talked with Eddie.

Eddie was Lithuanian, but had been born in America. His father had come to America in 1906, and married Eddie's mother in 1917. Eddie was born in 1919. His parents were homesick and returned to Lithuania when Eddie was four years old. In 1947 all American citizens, which Eddie's family was, were extracted and sent "home." In Eddie's case, it meant he was sent to a foreign home. He was an engineer, educated in Germany and the U.S., had a good job with Johnson & Johnson, and was very good looking. He was eleven years older than Donna.

"You got a boyfriend?" Eddie asked. Donna shook her head.

"What about you and Katie? Are you serious?" she asked.

"Kate? She isn't serious about too much. I'm not, though. I'm Catholic. Kate's Protestant and pretends that doesn't matter. But it matters to my family and to me. When I'm serious with a girl, it will be a Lithuanian, a Catholic girl."

Donna couldn't control the shiver than wiggled through her.

They dated for three years. Kate never spoke to her favorite friend again. But, Donna didn't care. She knew this was the man she'd waited for all her life.

At the Church of the Nativity in Chicago, with her sister beside her as her maid of honor, Donna married Eddie, the man she chose for herself. She imagined a blissful life of love, laughter, and a large family. Joy would now be hers, forever.

Chapter 45

Happily Ever After

Eddie's elderly father was alone. His wife had died, and now Eddie was married. Eddie brought the elderly, obese diabetic man to live with them, for Donna to care for.

She cared lovingly for the old man before going to work, coming home over lunch to feed him, and hurrying home after work to tend to his needs.

They were all overjoyed when Donna discovered she was pregnant. Her joy was short lived when she developed toxemia. The twin baby girls died during a Caesarean delivery. She cried more than she ever thought possible. In the hospital room, which she shared with a woman who had just given birth to her fourth daughter, she railed at God.

"What is this about? Why have you done this to me?" she demanded. The other woman's husband came to visit his wife complaining loudly that it was "just another girl." Donna sobbed hysterically for days. She tried not to hear the woman's infant cry and suckling noises. *The joy should be mine. Why do I deserve this? Why, God, would you do this to me and Eddie? Are we not your faithful servants?*

Deep in depression and feeling very alone, she stayed home from work for one month. She was supposed to be resting, but she cared for Eddie's father and buried her depression in his needs. She left her job at Hart, Shaffner and Marx. *How can I face their questions? See their pity. Hear them blame me?* When she went to work at an insurance agency she asked to work in the dividends department where she'd be alone in a solitary office. *I don't want to endure questions, or listen to stories and look at pictures of other people's children. I don't want to hear their pity or their advice.*

A year later when she was pregnant again, she immediately quit work to stay home. Though she still cared for Eddie's father, she was determined to also take care of herself. When her car was rear-ended in the last month of her pregnancy, her back was seriously injured. The doctor said they could only wait and see. She developed toxemia, but baby John was delivered Caesarean, a healthy, live baby. Donna thanked God and never returned to work outside her home. Eddie, John, and Eddie's father were Donna's world.

In 1968, her prayers were answered and she was pregnant again. Eddie paced and the doctor worried. Her legs were swollen twice the normal size, and her nose bled profusely for three straight days. The nun on the obstetrics floor sat at Donna's bedside for hours at a time praying, knitting, and talking to God, chatting as if He were in the room with them. A second son, Andrew, was born, in spite of the overwhelming complications and the doctor's grim prognosis.

For the next 24 years Donna nursed her father-in-law and raised her two boys. She also shared the care of her ailing mother with her brothers and sisters for intervals of three months at a time until her mother's death in 1975.

Since Donna was one of the few mothers in her neighborhood who didn't work outside the home, she often found herself caring for neighbor children who popped in, or were sent to her after school. She provided them with cookies, Band-Aids, help with homework, and even birthday parties.

Donna and Eddie lived in an ethnic neighborhood with a lot of police and city workers. It reminded her of her early years in Kaunas when all the children knew all the neighbors and everyone felt safe sitting and playing on the front steps. Adults were comfortable embracing or disciplining all the neighborhood children. She could wave to the air, and someone who knew her would wave back.

The neighbors watched as Donna cared for the two old sick people, her own two hearty boys, and all the kids in the neighborhood who traipsed in and out of her spotless house, while her husband's job kept him on the road. They watched her repair her roof, shovel the snow, cut the grass, wash the windows, repair the steps and paint the walls. The standard response to any whining in her neighborhood was, "Look, if Donna can do it, so can you!"

In 1983, Johnson & Johnson moved to New Jersey. Donna's and Eddie's sons were both away in college. Donna moved Eddie's failing 96 year-old father into a nursing facility. She visited him three times a day to be sure he was properly fed and clean. Eddie retired from Johnson & Johnson, and his father died. It was a year of upheaval and change.

The empty nesters decided to move to a smaller home in a warmer climate for the next phase of their life. Donna had tried two years to convince Eddie he'd love Florida, but once they were settled in Port St. Lucy, he declared it was the best move ever. Eddie became a serious biker often bicycling fifty miles a day. They both enjoyed good health and the out of doors. They traveled to Europe visiting Norway, Sweden, Russia, and Italy. Donna had her heart set on visiting Spain. These were happy years of retirement; finally they were devoted to just each other.

Vytas and Donna 1990s

Chapter 46

Getting Away

At age 83, Eddie complained of shoulder pain. Within months he was unable to get up. An MRI showed a tumor on his spine. After eleven treatments Donna brought him home to a hospital bed and a room full of equipment. Their sons came home and the priest visited with the sacraments. The priest told Donna to talk to Eddie.

"These semi-comatose patients can often hear," he said. She told Eddie how much she loved him and would see him again. He opened his eyes, spoke to her, and died peacefully.

Donna cried a lake full of tears. She had worked in bookkeeping and accounting for years, in charge of major finance departments. But suddenly she couldn't balance her own check book. She felt so dumb, so bewildered. The bills were all in Eddie's name. She was buried in paper work that should have been easy for her. Insurance forms that had been so familiar to her, things she'd helped others with for years, now confused and upset her. She sold their house to the city for their road-widening project. She went through it all as if in a fog. Just when she thought she had control, someone said the word "widow" and she fell apart all over again. She would see the word written on a document: *Widow*, and cry hysterically for hours.

A year later on the first anniversary of Eddie's death, Donna decided she needed to get away. She wanted to go somewhere quiet, somewhere no one knew her or Eddie. She wanted to go where she wouldn't need to be a "couple," somewhere families didn't gather to laugh and play together. She wanted to see some place different, try something new, get a grip on her emptiness; maybe see a new part of the country, try to get reenergized.

The picture in the magazine looked idyllic; just what she had in mind. The town was Cashiers, North Carolina. She'd never heard of it. She looked on the internet for the listings of inns in that town and found The Millstone Inn. It looked perfect. She packed her suitcase.

She sat on the edge of the bed at The Millstone Inn. *Now what? Here you are. Now what?*

"Cute little phonebook," she said aloud to herself. "It isn't even a quarter of the size of the Chicago phone directory. And not as big as Port St. Lucy, either."

She thumbed through the pages looking for places to go, things to see, shops to peruse. As she always did when she visited a new place, she checked to see if anyone else with her name was on these pages. No. And then, with her finger scrolling down, she saw it. She hesitated. "It couldn't be. Could it?"

She opened the desk drawer to find a postcard with the inn's picture on it. She checked the address in the phone book, addressed the post card, and wrote the message. "Are you the same Vytas...

She signed her name, but without giving it any thought, she signed her married name, the name she'd used for the past twenty two years. A name Vytas had never heard.

Chapter 47

Postcard

Vytas bought a lot in Cashiers and started building a house in the woods for Aldona. They moved into their home Labor Day, 1990. He did all the finish work on the inside, and trim on the outside. He oversaw the entire construction. He created an old world look, like a folk tale from the forests of Lithuania. They lived quietly offering hospitality to friends. They were involved in the small parish church, created amazing gardens their neighbors enjoyed visiting, and walked the woodlands surrounding their home. A collection of Vytas's wood working projects adorned the house and gardens. It was a dream retirement for ten years.

Aldona's cancer was diagnosed in December 2001. Memorial Day 2002, Vytas found himself alone. She was buried in the small cemetery behind the church. He created a metal sculpture for her grave and lovingly tended the roses at the site every Sunday after Mass.

Vytas didn't cry much. His friends worried about him.

"He needs to grieve," they said.

"Dying is a natural thing," he answered them. "I'm sad she is no longer here, of course I am. Sure, I miss her. But, tears won't change that. I face that reality. Dying is part of life. It's what we do. We're born, we live, and we die. If you don't die, you just have to keep living."

As time went on, well-meaning friends wanted him to join grieving groups, support groups, and get out more.

"I don't need groups to grieve with me," he said. "I can grieve fine by myself. Why is everyone bugging me about this? Let me be. Dying is a natural thing. It's how it goes. We just go on. We just keep living."

"You need a dog, Vytas," his neighbors told him. "So you aren't lonely."

Vytas laughed. "I don't need a dog; I need a woman!" He enjoyed seeing the shocked looks on his friends' faces when he said this.

The previous April his neighbor had found a puppy at the front gate of their development. They kept him for the summer, but when they left for their home in Florida at the end of the summer the neighbors brought "Champ" to Vytas.

"The dog spends every day sunbathing on your porch anyway. So we are giving him to you."

"I'll have to think about it," Vytas answered. "I'll let you know. I'm not sure I want a dog. I'll let you know."

A few days later Vytas got a phone call.

"Good morning. This is the Cashiers Veterinarian Clinic. Your dog is ready to be picked up."

"My dog? What dog?"

"Why, Champ, of course. He's had his rabies shot and general annual check-up. He's in fine shape. The folks who dropped him off for you on their way out of town left his bed and bowl, leash and toys. They're all ready and waiting for you. You can come anytime."

Champ was a fun companion for Vytas. He was a big boisterous puppy, a black lab mixed with something else large and energetic. He chewed some things, but Vytas, the old farm boy, patiently waited him out.

"You'll grow out of it. You're a good companion, Champ. I like you fine; but, what we need is a woman in this house." The dog wagged his tail in a state of permanent delight.

"Oh, I see you agree with me, huh?"

Vytas knew a few widows through church and community and he hinted, but nothing came of it. His neighbor and long-time friend who hiked through

Vytas's gardens regularly, tried to pair him up with a Yugoslavian-German friend. He wasn't impressed.

Then, a post card arrived. "Are you the same Vytas who was in the resettlement camp in Germany?"

"Who is this person, Donna something or other? Never heard of her. You know her, Champ? Me either. She says she's recently a widow. Probably she wants my money." He tossed the postcard in the wastebasket and went back to his current wood working project.

Auld Lang Syne

Chapter 48

Vytas picked up on the third ring. A fourth ring and she would have hung up the phone, she was so nervous.

"Hello," he said. "Yes, that's right. It's me. Who is this? Who? *That* Donna? Oh, ja it's me, for sure. How's your brother?" They lapsed into Lithuanian and swam in a sea of memories.

And so the conversation went for the next hour, covering two families, two continents, and 35 years. Vytas invited her to lunch. She hesitated.

"Hmm. I really don't date," she said.

"It's not a date," he said. "It's lunch!"

When Donna first saw Vytas she stared. *How'd he get to be so old?*

"What are you looking at? I'm 74 years old, what did you expect?"

Donna smiled. "Well, I didn't know you would have no hair, and what you do have is white. I didn't think about that." *But you are still tall and handsome.*

"And you, what about your nice braids? I see you haven't any."

"Well, I'm 74, too. Braids are too much trouble, and I'm modern now, anyway. I cut them off years ago, and got a permanent." *He remembers I had braids?*

"You look nice to me," he said.

"I remember you as a kid, a stuck up boy who thought he was God's gift to girls. Now you are an old man. Are you still stuck up?"

"I'm not an old man, not yet; I'm just an older man," he laughed. "I remember you as a bossy and independent girl. I think maybe you still are. I never was stuck up, but maybe I'm still God's gift to women. Did you think so?" His blue eyes danced merrily.

"I'm still bossy and independent," she answered. *What is wrong with me. I'm shivering like a school girl. There is something about Vytas that is the same; something right. I feel safe with him. I like to be with him. I always have.*

Over lunch they talked more, realizing how much history they shared, even though they hadn't seen one another in 35 years. They sipped their coffee slowly.

"They all wanted me to have a dog," he told her with a twinkle in his eye. "I told them, I don't need

227

a dog, I need a woman. I want one with her own money and who knows how to clean fish."

Donna laughed at his joke, wondering if it was a joke after all.

"I'm not looking for romance, either," she said. "I have my own money, and I don't clean fish."

They wrote casual cards and notes to each other after Donna went back to Florida.

"Come to visit me when the leaves are changing," Vytas wrote. "It's very nice here."

In October, Donna accepted his invitation, telling no one where she was going, and certainly not that she'd be visiting a man.

"What would they think?" she huffed. "And I'm not staying with him. I'll stay at the Millstone Inn." *When did I start talking to myself?*

"You are right. The mountains are beautiful in the fall. I'm glad I came," she said.

"I remember you," he said, "I admired you. Mostly I thought of you as the sister of Kent and Victor. But I liked you."

"You never even noticed me!"

"Yes, I did. You weren't a silly gossip like the other girls. You were a girl with self-confidence and I admired that."

"Vytas, I never thought you even knew who I was. You were my first crush."

"Me?"

"Uh huh. Tall, good looking, and so much a leader. If you liked me, why didn't you ever keep company with me? We never danced or walked together. But I know you went out with girls. You went with my best friend. You had a date with my dress once, though. She was wearing it."

"I was just a young boy, Donna, I couldn't ask you. I only asked out girls I didn't care about. I was too afraid of rejection to ask someone I cared about. It's how it is when you're a young boy." He sipped his coffee.

Donna stared at him over her mug. She smiled. "Well, I never knew that." They shared the twists and turns of their lives. The waitress refilled their cups several times.

"I like you," he said. "I'd like you to stay."

"Vytas, I can't stay with you. What will people say? How can we go to church together when your friends will say we are 'shaked up.'"

"It's called shacked up. And that's not what we're doing. My friends don't mind my business anyway. I think we're old enough to know what's right and what's not. Donna, for goodness sake, are you blushing like a school girl?"

"I've always been square, Vytas. I guess I still am. But, I always wished you would hold my hand. I still do. But, I'm too old for a crush. Do you think this is disrespectful? To Eddie and to Aldona, I mean." He reached across the table and took her hand.

"I think it is the ultimate compliment."

"How so?"

"If someone had an unhappy marriage or miserable time at being married, would they ever want to do it again? You and I, we were so fortunate, we married good people we loved and who loved us. We had happy marriages; so of course, we want to have that again. That is a compliment to our deceased spouses. That's what I think."

"Yes, I think you are right. Do you think we might speak to your priest about it?"

"We can talk to him. I'll call Father Bill in the morning."

"We want to live together now, we want to do it the right way, and be married," Vytas explained to the priest. "We both had good marriages and we both want to be married again."

"You are paying a compliment to your deceased spouses. You were both happy or you wouldn't want to do this. I know you both loved your spouses. And now you can also love each other. God will continue to bless you," the priest said.

Donna smiled and rolled her eyes toward Vytas. "I think I heard that before. Are you two in cahoots? But, I need the independence of having my own money, the peace of mind that comes from knowing I can always support myself." Donna added. "If we marry, I will lose that income."

"I see," said the priest, "and I understand. I hear that a lot. You, and many older couples like you, are between a rock and hard place. But, this is what we can do." The priest laid out his plan, which satisfied Donna, Vytas, and the Church.

Vytas and Donna were married in 2005, in the small parish of St. Jude Catholic Church in Cashiers, North Carolina. Along with Champ, they reside in the home Vytas built and has lived in since 1990. Their parallel lives brought them half way around the world as survivors of a war, immigrants, spouses in happy marriages, lonely survivors, to find themselves in love again, ready for the next phase of their lives together.

"Now, we'll see what God has in store for us next," Donna said with a smile.

"It will be good, we'll see," he answered.

The Millstone Inn property where Donna wrote the postcard to Vytas is only about 200 yards from the home where Vytas received it. Another bit of irony in their story concerns the American army intelligence officer who was sent to their resettlement camp in Hanau, Germany, to investigate the refugee situation. His name was Al Cameron from Clemson, South Carolina. In later years he also retired to Cashiers and became a friend of Vytas and Donna. He passed away at home in 2011.

One must believe there was Divine Direction in the lives of Donna and Vytas, who are no longer between a rock and a hard place, but living comfortably in their golden years, unafraid, not alone, and praising God for their wonderful lives.

Lithuania's Children

Lithuania began protesting openly in 1987 for her independence. A wall dividing East Germany and West Germany, put in place at the end of the war and known as the Berlin Wall, finally came down June 27, 1989. With the removal of the wall, the communist stronghold on the small nations began to loosen. With support of the free world, in 1990, Lithuania bravely declared her independence. She was the first of the Soviet republics to do so. A Soviet crackdown killed 13 more civilians in 1991, but in August 1991, Lithuania finally won her independence.

Today the Lithuanians are governed by a new constitution based on western principles. They continue to work to strengthen their democratic institutions and create a competitive free-market economy while continuing to develop and preserve their inherent culture for future generations of Lithuanian children. They have a high Human Development Index and the fastest growing economics in the European Union. Every year in February they celebrate the Act of Independence Day commemorating the signing of the Act of Independence. They continue to campaign against socialist and liberal policies especially ethical questions.

And like Vytas and Donna, Lithuania is no longer alone and afraid.

Rock and a Hard Place

Shari Parker Publishing
2785 CR 3103
New Boston, Texas 75570
903-933-6273
sharipar@yahoo.com
www.shariparkerpublishingandprinting.com